THE ELECTIONS HANDBOOK

*A guide for candidates, voters
and electoral staff*

Ron Kendall

Fitzwarren Publishing

©Fitzwarren Publishing 2001

First published in 1996
Second edition 2001

British Library Cataloging in Publication Data
A CIP record for this book is available from the British Library.

ISBN 0-9524812 0 0

Published by:
Fitzwarren Publishing,
2 Orchard Drive, Aston Clinton, Aylesbury, Bucks HP22 5HR

Printed in England by Halstan & Co. Ltd

CONTENTS

Preface

i

6. Counting the votes

7. Election expenses

8. Polling agents

9. Counting agents

10. Secrecy of the vote

11. Election petitions

tions 39; Respondent to the petition 39; The presentation of the petition 40; Security for the costs of a petition 40; Trial of the election petition 40; House of Commons Disqualification Act 1975 41.

12. Register of electors

Publication of register of electors 42; Dates of publication 42; Supply of computer data and labels 42; The right to register as an elector 42; Qualifying date 43; Declaration of local connection 43; List of Commonwealth Countries 43; Dealing with those reluctant to register 44.

13. Canvassing

The first canvas 45; Recruiting canvassers 45; How canvassers should operate 45; Some tips for canvassers 47; Questions canvassers are frequently asked 48.

14. Assistance

Assistance for people with disabilities 51; Postal or proxies for people with disabilities 51; People in business 51; Overseas electors 52.

15. Armed forces

Registration of service personnel 54; Postal and proxy votes for service personnel 54; Registration Index 54.

16. Data Protection Act and Junk Mail

The introduction of the Act 56; Data users 56; Non public information 56; Purchase of data 56; The effect of the Act on political parties 57; Junk mail and how to stop it 57.

17. Parish & Community elections

Parish and local government elections 58; The procedure for parish and community elections 58; Casual vacancies 59.

18. Combined elections

19. Representation of the People Act 2000

Statutory and legal sources and further reading

Electoral regions

Glossary

Index

Specimen forms

PREFACE

Ron Kendall was chief registration officer from the end of 1983 until his retirement in December 1998. He was involved in the organisation of all types of elections including Berkshire County Council elections, those for Reading Borough Council and parliamentary elections for the Reading East and Reading West constituencies.

He was also co-ordinator for the European parliamentary elections in the Thames Valley constituency, which consisted of the Borough of Reading, Bracknell Forest District Council, Newbury District Council, Wokingham District Council, the Royal Borough of Windsor and Maidenhead, Slough Borough Council and Spelthorne Borough Council.

On occasions local schools have asked him for assistance in staging mock elections. It was his policy always to provide as much guidance as possible. It is partly with schools that conduct such mock elections in mind that this book was written.

Below is a letter received from one of the schools where, with Ron's help, mock elections were held.

Dear Mr Kendall,
I am writing to thank you, as I was unable to thank you in person when I returned the ballot box, stamp etc. this afternoon. It was very kind of you to give me so much help and to loan so much material to make the mock election as real as possible.
It was a very successful event for our senior pupils and I am sure that they all learned a great deal about democracy from it. Our winning candidate became Head teacher for the day as I had decided against running the election on party political lines. He thoroughly enjoyed his day but was unable to fulfil his election promises to the pupils and so another facet of realism was introduced.
Thank you once again for all your help.
Head of Pre-vocation

When "poll tax" was introduced in 1990 many authorities saw the electoral registration figures drop drastically. Extra effort and hard work was required by electoral registration teams to bring the figures back to pre-poll tax levels. A strong and efficient canvassing team is the best way to achieve this revival. Ron believed that a book such as this would assist many involved in the canvassing process.

The guidance contained within this book will also be of assistance to prospective candidates and their agents. There will be questions that candidates, particularly those new to elections, would like to be able to answer for themselves. Candidates may be unable to do so because the necessary books are not available to them or are too expensive. Within this handbook Ron sets out to explain in detail, without too much legal jargon, the procedure for the election from nomination, to the counting of the votes and subsequently the election of the successful candidate.

Part of the text concerns the registration of the electorate and their right and the method of voting at the various types of election.

Richard Taylor
Returning Officer
Reading Borough Council.

Author's notes

I apologise for the use of "he" in gender-neutral situations. I am merely following a grammatical convention rather than expressing any inherent sexism.

I am grateful to many people for the assistance they have given to me in producing this book. These include Richard Taylor, the returning officer of Reading Borough Council; Liz Cloke, who replaced me at Reading Borough Council; Daphne Gray, Registration Services Manager for Bracknell Forest Borough Council; Steve Kendall, my son, for his assistance in compiling the contents and index; and lastly to Norman Church, for his in-depth report on canvassing methods.

Generally I have stated the law as it stood on 31 May 2000 but have added changes brought about by the Representation of the People Act 2000, in force from 16th February 2001.

Ron Kendall.

A SHORT HISTORY OF ELECTIONS

It was not until the thirteenth century that it became the practice for the Sovereign to summon a Parliament. One of the main instigators of the change towards parliamentary government, rather than complete royal control, was Simon De Montfort, Earl of Leicester. It was he who, as one of a number of barons and subjects of King Henry III angry at what was happening in the country at the king's hands, demanded change.

At the time - around 1250 - the Magna Carta's provisions were being ignored and the cost of some of Henry's schemes, such as the rebuilding of Westminster Abbey and a proposed scheme to make one of his younger sons King of Sicily, led to dismay and rebellion. The barons were led by Simon De Montfort, who was said to be the most outstanding English personality of his day. The barons tried to gain some control over the King with a permanent council (Provisions of Oxford 1258) to supervise his actions.

A conference held in 1264 was followed by a much larger parliament in January 1265. The parliament formed then fashioned the roots of democratic government which still exist to this day.

But the passage of democracy was not an easy one. Civil War broke out in 1264 as Henry opposed moves which he felt diminished his divine power. Ultimately, the King and his son Edward were defeated and Simon governed England by military dictatorship.

Prince Edward, however, escaped and led a royalist army to Evesham, against Simon De Montfort. Simon was killed along with most of his supporters. His body was decapitated and dismembered, his remains interred at Evesham Abbey, later to be exhumed and scattered to prevent public veneration.

However, the cause he lived for did not die with him. Ruling as King Edward I, Henry's III's son accepted that there was a need for democratic government. Despite further arguments and bloodshed, democracy was established in Britain. By the end of the thirteenth century, each sheriff had the responsibility of returning the writs upon which they had to enter the names of people who were to serve in parliament. (This was probably the origin of the name returning officer.) At the time there was no prescribed method for selection and the sheriffs exercised their own discretion.

The Parliamentary Elections Act 1695 was an attempt to regulate the sheriffs' returns and it was this Act that introduced the rule - still in force today - prohibiting anyone under the age of twenty-one from being eligible to be elected to parliament. Meanwhile, the poll was still being conducted by the counting of heads (the word poll means 'head'). The passing of the Ballot Act 1872 ensured that henceforth ballots would be secret. It was also this act that laid the ground rules for the conduct of returning officers, much of which remain in force today.

Anther important milestone in the election process was votes for women. Many might think this was a 20th century movement but in fact it was founded in the seventeenth century. A pioneer of the movement was Mary Wollstonecraft who produced her chief work on the subject of suffrage *A Vindication of the Rights of Women* in 1792. All efforts by women in the years that followed were opposed even by Queen Victoria, the reigning monarch of the early 19th century and her minister William Gladstone.

In 1903 the formerly timid policies of the Suffragettes changed when Emmeline Pankhurst led a militant faction and employed tactics of window breaking, bombing, picketing and other such aimed at disruption against anti-suffragist legislation. In 1913 one of the Suffragettes threw herself to her death under the horses' hooves of the Epsom Downs' Derby.

Through the efforts of these brave women, many of whom suffered rough handling by police and were jailed and fined for their beliefs, the law was eventually changed. Because of them and others like them in many of the countries of the world by the 1980s women almost everywhere could vote.

The function of the sheriff was changed with the Representation of the People Act 1983. Although in county constituencies the sheriff remains nominally the returning officer his functions are now purely formal. Acting returning officers - usually the electoral registration officer of the borough and returning officer in their own right for local elections - now take charge of most aspects of the elections.

Registration officers are local government employees and should not be appointed as a result of any political patronage. On the other hand returning officers are often so appointed. Many are mayors of the areas which coincide or overlap with the constituencies for whom they act as returning officers.

2

THE ELECTION CANDIDATE

Parliamentary Elections

After the dissolution of Parliament or upon a casual vacancy occurring (which could be the resignation or death of an MP) a writ is issued. After the issue of the writ, anyone who can satisfy the qualification requirement may declare himself to be an independent candidate or can be nominated by another person or political party by whom they have been adopted.

Qualifications for candidature

A nominee must be twenty-one years of age on the day of nomination and a Commonwealth citizen or citizen of the Republic of Ireland.

Local Government Elections

A candidate for local government may be nominated either as an independent or adopted by a political party. If successful, the candidate will serve on the local council (usually for a period of four years). A candidate nominated to fill a casual vacancy (which may occur due to a resignation or death of a councillor) would be elected only for the remaining term of the retiring or deceased councillor.

Qualifications for candidature:

A nominee must be twenty-one years of age on the day of nomination and a Commonwealth citizen, citizen of the Republic of Ireland or a citizen of the European Union, and:

a) be a local government elector for the area of the authority; or

b) have during the whole of the twelve months preceding the day on which he is nominated occupied as owner or tenant land or other premises in the area of the authority; or

c) have had his principal or only place of work in the area of the authority in the twelve months preceding the day on which he is nominated; or

d) have resided in the area during the whole twelve months preceding the day on which he is nominated

In parish elections, a candidate must also live within 4.8 kilometres of the parish.

A candidate's duties

A candidate has a duty to complete the consent to nomination and deliver it with the nomination paper or deliver it within one month before the last day for delivering nomination papers. Failure to fulfil this delivery requirement will invalidate the nomination. The consent must contain a statement signed by a witness, declaring that the candidate is qualified to be elected on the day of election.

An election agent must be appointed by the candidate, to act on his behalf in all matters connected to his election. If an election agent is not appointed the candidate will be deemed to be his own agent. A candidate at an election of parish councillors need not have an election agent.

The candidate should read the notes regarding secrecy, particularly if it is his intention to visit the polling stations or attend the counting of the votes. He should also bear in mind his responsibility to help maintain the secrecy of the ballot. He must make the required deposit in cash or banker's draft or as specified by the returning officer. This applies to parliamentary and European elections only. In local government elections no deposit is required. At parliamentary elections the deposit is £500 and at European parliamentary elections it is £1000.

The candidate and his election agent must make the required declaration of election expenses on the correct form and within the time notified by the returning officer. A late entry can disqualify a successful candidate. Even an unsuccessful candidate is still committing an offence if the return is not submitted within the required time. The returning officer will inform the Crown Prosecutor if a candidate makes a late return or has exceeded the allowed limit of election expenses. Even if no money is spent on an election campaign a nil return is still required.

Disqualification from election

A person may not stand in an election if he holds a paid office under the particular local authority he seeks to represent or he holds a politically restricted post. Bankrupts cannot be elected, nor can anyone disqualified under any enactment relating to corrupt or illegal practices, or anyone who has been sentenced to a term of imprisonment of three months or more without the option of a fine during the five years up to and including the year of election. This applies whether the term of imprisonment was suspended or not.

A candidate found guilty of corrupt electoral practices such as bribery, using undue influence or impersonation of a voter or voters, is disqualified from standing for election in the constituency in which he committed the offences for a period of ten years or in another constituency for five years. If the election agent was at fault the candidate would be disqualified for seven years.

Nomination of candidates: parliamentary elections

Once Parliament is dissolved there are of course no sitting Members of Parliament. Candidates who were MP's before the dissolution of Parliament should not refer to themselves as MP's on their nomination papers, although it is permissible for them to convey the fact that they were previously MP for the constituency.

A candidate is permitted to present more than one nomination paper to the returning officer. If the first paper fails, another can then be substituted. It should be noted however that no elector should subscribe to more than one of those papers. The returning officer is only concerned with the validity of the nomination papers and should only declare a paper invalid for one of the following reasons:

a) that the particulars of the candidate or those subscribing to the paper are not as required by law; or

b) that the paper is not subscribed to as required; or

c) that the candidate is disqualified by the Representation of the People Act 1981.

Nomination of candidates: local government elections

Each candidate must be nominated on a separate nomination paper. The paper must be signed by a proposer, a seconder, and eight people who support his application

All the people signing the paper must be local government electors for the ward and their electoral numbers must be given on the nomination paper together with the distinctive letter or letters from their record in the electoral register. If anyone knowingly or unknowingly subscribes to more than one nomination paper either as proposer, seconder or as an assentor, it will be the first paper only received by the returning officer which will be accepted. Any others will be rejected. Candidates therefore should ask assentors if they have already subscribed to any other paper.

For parish elections a proposer and seconder only are required.

The completed paper must be delivered to the place indicated on the notice of election, usually the returning officer's council address. The nomination paper must give the full names of the candidate (surname first) and the home address of the candidate. A fault as minor as entering names in the wrong order would invalidate the paper. Someone known by another name or nickname may have this added to the nomination - for instance "Brown, James (otherwise known as Jim)". This entry would be written under the first names in the box provided rather than in the description box.

Under the Register of Political Parties Act 1998 a candidate standing for election in the name of a registered party must produce a certificate issued by the registered nominating officer of that party. A candidate can, if he does not represent any political party, insert "Independent" in his nomination or insert no description at all.

Consent to nomination

The nomination of any candidate is not valid unless the candidate's consent is given in writing on the correct form. It must be delivered with the nomination or within one month before the last day for delivering nomination papers.

The consent must contain a statement declaring that on the day of nomination the candidate was and on the day of election will be, qualified to be elected (giving particulars of the qualification). The statement must also be signed by a witness.

Withdrawal from candidature

A candidate may withdraw his candidature providing the withdrawal notice is delivered not later than the sixteenth day before the day of election to the place fixed for delivery of nomination papers. He must sign it himself and have it attested by one witness.

If the candidate is outside the UK, the notice of withdrawal may be signed by his proposer and must be accompanied by a signed declaration also signed by the proposer. It will have the same effect as if signed by the candidate.

If the candidate is nominated by more than one paper it must be accompanied by a declaration signed by all of the proposers unless any of them are outside the UK, in which case the fact that they are outside the UK should be recorded on the form. If a candidate is validly nominated for more than one electoral area he must withdraw from all but one of those areas. If he does not do this he will be deemed to have withdrawn from all of the areas.

A candidate's rights during the election

The candidate has a right to attend the opening of postal votes. This right is rarely exercised due to the time taken. The opening of the postal votes can start before the count proper begins - sometimes as early as 5.00 pm, some four hours before the count itself.

The candidate has the right to visit the polling station but upon doing so must conduct himself in a manner that will not disrupt the election. If he does not conduct himself in a proper manner the presiding officer may order that he leave. During such a visit a candidate may use a copy of the register of electors and may mark it in any way to determine who has voted but the register should not be taken out of the polling station. The register should be deposited with the presiding officer.

Any candidate in a parliamentary or European parliamentary election is entitled to send free of charge one unaddressed postal communication, containing matter relating to the election not exceeding 60 grams in weight, to each address in the constituency or one such communication addressed to every elector. He is also entitled, free of any postal charges, to send one communication to everyone in the list of proxies.

There is no such arrangement for local government elections.

A candidate at parliamentary or European parliamentary elections is entitled to use a suitable room in school premises free of charge (although he must pay for heating, lighting and cleaning and any damage to the property) at reasonable times (that is, when the school is not functioning as an educational establishment) to hold public meetings for the purpose of promoting his candidature. This right does not extend to the use of sixth form colleges. Reasonable notice must be given to any school, where it is intended to hold a meeting of this nature.

For a parliamentary or European parliamentary election the right exists only between the receipt of writ and the day preceding the day of election.

For a local election, the right exists between the last day for publication of the notice of election and the day before election day. In the event of there not being a school available in the area of the election or the constituency the candidate has the right to use a school outside the area. The same rules apply regarding reasonable notice.

Some Frequently Asked Questions

Candidates at local elections are often unfamiliar with the law relating to elections. The same could be said of many of the election agents to whom electoral law can be a maze. Set out below are some of the many and varied questions that a candidate or an election agent is likely to ask.

Q. What will I need to do first if I am to put myself up for election as an independent local councillor?
A. You will need a nomination paper, consent to nomination and if appointing an agent, you will need an appointment of agent form.

Q. Where can I obtain these forms?
A. The returning officer or his staff will provide them free of

charge.

Q. What if I don't have an election agent?

A. In that case you will be deemed to be your own agent. This will also be the case if you don't appoint an agent by the specified time. For parish elections, you don't need to appoint an election agent.

Q. Who should complete the forms - my agent or me?

A. You can complete them yourself but most of the work in obtaining the signatures would normally be undertaken by the election agent.

Q. How many signatures will I need?

A. One proposer, one seconder and eight others to sign your nomination. All must be electors within the ward in which you are standing.

For parish elections, proposer and seconder only are required.

Q. Can these be members of my own family?

A. Yes.

Q. I have heard that the names have to be printed on the nomination paper as well as the signatures. Is that correct?

A. The normal signature is all that is required, but it will help the returning officer and his staff if the names are also printed.

Q. Where are the assentors' names published?

A. Only on the notice of poll, but the names of the proposer and seconder are also included on the statement of nominations.

Q. Am I required to complete the consent to nomination?

A. Yes, it must be submitted to the returning officer at the same time as you submit your nomination paper, or within one month before the last day for delivery of nomination papers. The nomination will be invalid without it.

Q. What about the agent's appointment?
A. If you are appointing an agent, this must be made on the appropriate form. However, it does not have to be submitted at the same time as the nomination. For parish elections you need not appoint an agent.

Q. If I make a mistake on the paper what should I do?
A. Contact the returning officer who will issue you with another one

Q. Where can I obtain these forms?
A. The returning officer or his staff will provide them free of charge.

Q. How old do I have to be before I can put myself up for election?
A. Twenty-one on the day of nomination.

Q. I would like to put myself up for election as a candidate for one of the major parties. How would I go about this?
A. All of the major political parties have their own methods of adopting their candidates. Contact one of them for information.

Q. As a candidate am I allowed to have a copy of the register of electors?
A. All candidates are issued with a free copy of the register of electors for the ward in which they are to stand.

Q. What about postal vote lists. Am I allowed to have those?
A. When the lists are printed, any candidate requesting a copy will be supplied with one free of charge. Data on disk or tape can also be requested and will be free of charge.

Q When can I submit my nomination paper to the returning officer?

A. On or before the specified date as printed on the timetable that you will be given by the returning officer or his staff. You should take the documentation to the election administrator as soon as you have it ready. The administrator can then check the paperwork before it is submitted to the returning officer. If you leave it until the last day and there are errors you may not have time to correct them.

Q. When do I have to start recording election expenses?
A. As soon as you have declared yourself to be a candidate, have been nominated, or adopted as a candidate or have appointed an election agent, whichever comes first.

Q. How can I find out who voted at the election?
A. The marked copies of the register of electors are available for inspection for up to six months after the date of the election by any candidate or agent who asks to view them.
For local elections, parish, and European elections, the copies are held by the local authority. In the case of parliamentary elections, the registers are delivered to the Clerk of the Crown.

Q. When do I have to send in my return of election expenses?
A. For local elections, the return must be made within 35 days after the result of the election is declared. In computing this date all days are included. (See 'dies non' defined in Glossary) In parish elections, the returns of candidates expenses must be submitted within 28 days (not computed) of the declaration of result of notice of poll.

Q. Do I have to return my declaration at the same time as my election agent returns his?
A. No, the candidate's declaration can be made up to seven days after the agent has returned all the expenses and the agent's declaration.

Q. When I have completed my declaration of expenses, how do I find a Justice of the Peace to sign them?
A. If you are a member of a political party and have an election agent, he will usually know of a JP who can help. If however you are not able to obtain the services of a JP do not delay returning your forms - the returning officer or the mayor of a council can usually sign the declaration in the absence of a JP.

At parliamentary, European parliamentary or parish elections most of the above answers would still apply, but would be amended to suit the particular election. For instance, the number of assentors to a European parliamentary election nomination is twenty-eight and at a parish election only a proposer and seconder are required.

Declaration of acceptance of office
After the result of the election, every successful candidate must make a declaration of acceptance of office on the prescribed form and witnessed by a returning officer or proper officer of the council or someone duly qualified.

The declaration of acceptance of office of a parish councillor must be made before or at the first meeting after election. After that the declaration can only be made if alternative arrangements have been approved at the first meeting after election. If the declaration is not made then, or if alternative arrangements are not approved at the first meeting after election there is no way in which a declaration can lawfully be made.

3

ELECTION AGENTS

Election agent's appointment

Every candidate, except in parish or community elections, must appoint an election agent who must have an office, the address of which has to be declared to the returning officer. The candidate may appoint only one such agent. A candidate may be his own election agent. The agent must be named no later than the time allowed for notices of withdrawal of candidature. The agent may be paid.

Sub-agent appointments

An election agent at a parliamentary election for a county constituency may appoint a sub-agent to act in any part of the constituency. Any act undertaken by the sub-agent will be taken as carried out by the election agent including any illegal act or default for which the agent or the sub-agent is liable to punishment.

The appointment of a sub-agent must be declared to the returning officer no later than the second day before the day of election. The name and address and office of any sub-agents so appointed will be made public. A sub-agent appointment is made by the election agent and not by the candidate and it should be submitted to the returning officer in writing.

Election agents' duties

The main duty of an election agent is to do everything in his power and within the letter of the law, to secure his candidate's success in the election. The agent will also pay any debts accrued and authorised by the candidate.

It should be borne in mind that a successful election depends on the return of election expenses being correct. Other candidates may inspect them or take extracts from them after they are lodged with the returning officer. Election expenses incurred are not enforceable against a candidate unless made by himself or the election agent.

Agents should ensure they obtain receipts in respect of any expenses. (See chapter 7 - Expenses)

Revocation of appointment of election agent

An election agent's appointment may be revoked but the Representation of the People Act 1983 requires that another agent be appointed forthwith. The name and address of the new agent must then be declared in writing to the returning officer. The death of an election agent has the same effect as revocation for the purposes of the Act.

4

RETURNING OFFICERS
(and Acting Returning Officers or deputies)

The returning officer is responsible for the conduct of any election. He must ensure that everything is done according to the Representation of the People Acts and other regulations.

In practice, returning officers normally have control over local elections in their own right. When, however, a parliamentary election takes place, they hand the responsibility over to acting returning officers. For county elections they hand over to deputy returning officers, although the practice for county elections ceased in most authorities with the introduction of unitary authorities when borough councils took over from county councils.

An acting returning officer (usually the mayor of a borough or a sheriff of a county) will, in a parliamentary election, hand the responsibility over to another officer. (in practice it could be the borough electoral registration officer who would probably also be the returning officer in his own borough) He will assume the responsibility of the election and make the return to The Clerk of the Crown.

If a returning officer or acting returning officer were found to be guilty of any breach of duty, he would face a penalty of a fine not exceeding level 5 or imprisonment for a term not exceeding 2 years or both. If, for example, at a local election there were a discrepancy between the published voting figures at the count and the possible votes on the basis of ballot papers, an inspection of the votes cast for each candidate would be carried out by a court. If subsequently the court found that there had been grave dereliction of duty, the returning officer might well be found guilty of an offence and sentenced as above.

Should a strike or industrial action by local authority staff mean that the returning officer could not fully despatch his duties leading to some of the regulations not being fully complied with he would not be in breach of his official duties and no offence would be committed.

He is not obliged to use council staff to run the election although he usually will do so. But in the event of industrial action he can use anyone to help him complete his tasks. Although clearly, returning officers would not want to do anything to upset industrial relations, they have a duty to conduct the election.

Returning officers can sometimes, where necessary, appoint deputy acting returning officers to assist them. These can have full powers or limited powers depending upon the circumstances of their appointment.

5

THE ELECTION TIMETABLE

Local government elections

The day of election is usually the first Thursday in May and can only be changed by the Secretary of State. The calculation of the dates for election purposes is made by starting with the day of the election and working backwards, the day before the election being day one. Excluded are weekends, bank holidays, Christmas Eve, Christmas Day, Boxing Day, Maundy Thursday, Good Friday, or a day appointed for thanksgiving or mourning. These days are archaically referred to as 'dies non'. Counting backwards to day twenty-five gives the date of the start of the election process (the notice of election).

The timetable for a local election is prepared well in advance of the election by the registration officer and is submitted to the returning officer for approval before being issued to candidates or election agents.

Publication of the notice of election

The publication of the notice of election is the first item on the local election timetable. It has to be published not later than the twenty-fifth day before the day of election and is displayed in as many locations as possible, in particular outside the polling stations.

Delivery of nomination papers

Nomination papers must be delivered to the returning officer not later than the nineteenth day before the day of election. The papers cannot be accepted before the date stated on the notice of election but early delivery is a wise precaution, as this will give the registration team the chance to check papers before they are submitted to the returning officer.

Each nomination paper must be accompanied by consent to nomination, duly signed by the candidate. The nomination paper is invalid without the consent form. However, the consent form can be delivered separately within one month before the last day for delivery of nomination papers.

Publication of statement of persons nominated

The statement of people nominated is prepared in the form of a notice with the full names and addresses of all the candidates, the ward in which they are standing, the description (if an independent candidate) or the name of the political party adopting them and the name of the candidate's proposer. This notice is put on public display by the returning officer no later than noon on the seventeenth day before the day of election.

Notice of withdrawal from candidature

A notice of withdrawal from candidature can only be accepted if it is submitted in writing before noon on the sixteenth day before the day of the election and signed by one witness.

Notice of appointment of election agents

The notice of appointment of election agents giving the name of the candidate and the home address and office of the election agent should be delivered to the returning officer no later than noon on the sixteenth day before the day of election. If it is received after this time, the candidate will be deemed to be his own election agent.

Applications to be treated as absent or proxy voters

An absent vote is another name for a vote by post and a proxy is someone appointed to act for the voter if for some reason the voter cannot get to the polling station in person. Applications to be an absent or proxy voter can be accepted by the returning officer. The application may be for an indefinite or a particular period.

An overseas elector is allowed to vote by proxy at parliamentary elections only.

Applications to be treated as absent voter - sudden changes in health or election employment

Applications to be treated as an absent voter because of a sudden change in health will be accepted no later than 5 p.m. on the sixth day before day of election. It has been used most frequently in the case of unforeseen hospitalisation or other ill health, preventing the applicant from attending the polling station.

This also applies to people whose official employment in connection with the election would prevent them voting in person. (Although candidates and other political workers would not fall under this provision)

Dispatch of postal ballot papers

The day for the dispatch of postal ballot papers is after 5 p.m. on the eleventh day before the date of the poll. In calculating the days, Saturday, Sunday, Christmas Eve, Christmas Day, Maundy Thursday, Good Friday, shall be disregarded.

Where a postal voter has not received the postal ballot paper by the fourth day before the day of the poll, they can apply to the returning officer for a replacement. Postage on all outgoing postal votes shall be prepaid with prepaid return envelopes for ballot papers posted within the United Kingdom.

Publication of notice of poll

The notice of poll takes the form of a poster. It contains the names and home addresses of all the candidates, the ward in which they are standing and the political party they represent and any other information listed on the nomination paper submitted to the returning officer. It must be displayed on or before the sixth day before the day of election.

Notice of appointment of polling or counting agents

Notice of appointment of polling or counting agents should be completed in the form of a letter and delivered to the returning officer before the fifth day before the day of the election.

Polling day

For local elections, polling will normally take place on the first Thursday in May each year. However, this can be altered if circumstances make it prudent to do so. (In 1986 local election polling day fell on the Jewish holiday of Shavuot so the election date was moved one week later to the second Thursday in May.)

Counting of the votes

The counting of the votes for a local government election usually takes place the same day as the election starts at 9.00 pm or as soon as the first of the ballot boxes reaches the count venue. All councils have their own method of arranging the count but still keep to the main framework of the various governing Acts of Parliament.

Submission of return and declaration of election expenses

Election expenses should be submitted to the returning officer within thirty-five days from the day of election, twenty-eight days for a parish election. (In the calculation of these days, 'dies non' are counted as normal days) This applies to any days after the event of an election. All declarations should be completed and monies accounted for on the return of election expenses form.

Particular attention should be paid to this exercise as the success of a candidate could depend on the return being correct as required by legislation.

Timetable for Parliamentary Elections

The method used to calculate the parliamentary elections timetable involves calculation forward from the proclamation. Nominations close six days from the date of proclamation and the timetable then progresses to nomination day. The day fixed for the poll is nomination day plus one to eleven days hence.

Counting the votes in Parliamentary and European Elections:

In parliamentary elections the starting time for counting votes is after the close of poll at 10.00 pm. The counting of the votes at a European parliamentary election differs from all other types of election in that no Member state can start the count proper until all the Member states of the European Union have closed their polls, which means that no one starts counting until the Sunday following the poll.

The only thing that is done immediately following the poll in a European election is the verification of the votes. This means that the quantity of papers in the boxes have to be checked and recorded on verification sheets and submitted to the acting returning officer by all the deputy acting returning officers making up the European constituency.

By-Elections:
Last day for receipt of parliamentary by-election nomination papers.
The last day for receipt of nomination papers in a parliamentary by-election is not earlier than the third day after the publication of the notice of election and no later than the seventh day after the receipt of the writ.

Day of poll in a parliamentary by-election
The day of the poll should be not earlier than the ninth nor later than the eleventh day after the last day for delivery of nomination papers.

Local government by-elections
A by-election (an election called to fill a casual vacancy which could be brought about by a councillor's resignation or death) is called by means of a notice in the form of a letter endorsed by two electors of the ward of the local authority and delivered to the returning officer.

At a local by-election the timetable for local government elections as described earlier in this chapter is used. Calculation of time differs however.

The by-election must be held within thirty-five days of written notice being received by the returning officer or proper officer of a local authority. Beginning Election Day, counted as day one, the days will be counted back to day twenty-five. The same rule applies regarding 'dies non' as in normal elections. If called within six months of normal local elections the by-election would be held at the same time as the local elections.

Suitable notices are posted declaring a casual vacancy as soon as such a vacancy is known to exist. The notice is in the form of a poster declaring that there is a casual vacancy to be filled and inviting nominations. A similar notice applies for a parliamentary seat as it does for local government wards.

6

THE COUNTING OF THE VOTES

Venue for the Count

Selecting the venue for the counting of the votes is entirely the responsibility of the returning officer. It need not be in the same electoral area and the votes do not have to be counted on the same day as the election but in practice that is usually the case. The venue will be provisionally booked by the election administrator well in advance - as much as a year before the election - and confirmed as soon as it is known the election will be contested.

Staffing the polling stations

Typically at local councils, lists are maintained of outside helpers who may also be used for delivery of registration forms and poll cards. A good registration officer will keep his eye out for any retiring staff within the council to ensure an ample number of people are available.

If a retired person has been a presiding officer or head counter, jobs which are the most difficult to fill because so much experience is required, so much the better. A personal approach is usually best, and gratefully received by those approached. Often retiring staff erroneously and modestly believe they will not be needed after retirement, so such people may not even bother to indicate a willingness to continue.

Towards the end of the February before May local elections, letters asking for volunteers are posted to all people on the outside helpers list. At the same time memos may be sent out to all departments in the Council asking for volunteers amongst staff. The replies will be sorted into those who can fulfil the roles of presiding officers, polling clerks and counting assistants.

There will usually be a surplus of polling clerks, some of whom if approached, will agree to have presiding officer training. After the training, although they cannot be promised a presiding officer appointment at once, they are usually quite pleased to continue as a polling clerk again if necessary. This sort of approach to the staffing problem usually produces the required result: the successful staffing of the polling stations.

However, there will always be cancellations for one reason or another. That is when careful advance planning by the registration officer will prove to be fruitful. The poll clerks trained as presiding officers can now be promoted and another poll clerk appointed to fill the resulting vacancy. The process is one that must be monitored carefully so that the numbers of poll clerks available and the number of those required at polling stations matches.

Under the present system there is no provision for reserve presiding officers A presiding officer works all day at a polling station, until the poll closes. That is the reason why poll clerks are trained to take over, should a presiding officer fall ill or fail to turn up at the station. There are usually more applications for poll clerk jobs than there are for presiding officers so a list is maintained and called upon should a problem arise.

When preparing the list of polling staff, there is a lot to be said for using husband and wife teams and ensuring these are not separated. Similarly other staff who know each other socially and are likely to be able to travel together should be accommodated in this way. An ability to car share helps the staff and in the long run is likely to benefit the registration officer too. The reasoning behind this is partly to save on travel expenses, but also because couples like to work together and may decline to take on the job if they are separated.

This should also be borne in mind when appointing counting staff who often share a car. In this case they should be put at the same table as they will not want to wait around for friends who are still counting after their ward is finished.

The In Charge counting assistant

It is good practice to send to the In Charge counting assistants a printed instruction sheet with their appointment letter as they do not always have time to digest the instructions before being thrown into the count. This is especially important when the In Charge counting assistant has not done the job before.

A periodic visit during the count by the administrator will be of benefit, too, as there will be many questions the inexperienced In Charge counting assistant is likely to ask.

Another good practice is to put new In Charge assistants at a table where there are experienced counters as these can often help, even though they may not want to do the job themselves. Most of the counting staff will arrive just before or after 9.00pm. If cheques are prepared in advance it might be useful to use the time before the votes are ready to be counted to pay counting staff. The ballot boxes should start to arrive about 9.20pm, at which time any keys to outside halls should be collected along with ballot paper accounts and expenses forms.

Ballot paper accounts

The ballot accounts should be deposited with the ballot box in the ward in which they are to be counted. The In Charge assistants should be approached early in the process (or as soon as it is thought that all the boxes are in) for confirmation that all boxes and ballot paper accounts appertaining to them are to hand.

Any missing at this stage of the proceedings can quickly be chased up if a list of all the presiding officers is at the count venue and marked with the relevant telephone numbers. A call to the presiding officer in question usually finds the missing papers.

People who may attend the count

Admittance cards to the count are sent to the candidates and their wives or husbands, their election agents, counting agents (the permitted numbers of which the returning officer will advise beforehand) and any other people permitted by the returning officer to attend. (this could include the local MP's or leaders of the political parties involved in the election)

A returning officer may admit more people if he is satisfied that the efficient counting of the votes will not be impeded and he has either consulted the election agents or thought it impractical to do so. The decision whether or not to give permission is one for the returning officer and provided he has consulted the election agents (or thought it impracticable to do so) he makes his own decision on the matter.

Even though they are consulted - and in the event of no election agent, a candidate is consulted - the election agents have no power to insist on their wishes being met.

Secrecy at the counting of the votes

The requirement of secrecy means that the returning officer has to issue to everyone attending the counting of the votes, a copy in writing of the provision of sub-sections 66 (1),(2), (3), and (6) of the Representation of the People Act 1983. These provisions concern the maintaining of secrecy of the voting and should be read carefully before attending the polling stations or at the counting of the votes.

Counting agents

Counting agents are those people appointed by the election agent, or the candidate acting as his own election agent, to oversee the counting of the votes. They are there merely to observe the counting and should not impede the counters by looking over their shoulders or speaking to the counters.

On no account should they touch the ballot papers or any of the other equipment of the count. They are there to satisfy themselves that the ballot papers have been correctly sorted and counted, allocated to the right candidate and nothing more.

The counting of the votes

The returning officer opens each ballot box in the presence of the counting agents and records the quantity of the ballot papers within and verifies this with the ballot paper account. This will include the postal ballot papers. Counting can start as soon as the ballot papers from one box can be put with those from another box.

Ballot papers to be counted face up

During the counting of the votes all papers should be kept face upwards, so that no one can see the numbers printed on the reverse of the paper. (The numbers correspond with the ballot paper numbers that are printed on the ballot paper counterfoil)

The only exception to this rule is when the verification of votes for a European parliamentary election takes place when votes are counted face down.

A typical notice of instruction to counting assistants

ANY BOROUGH COUNCIL
LOCAL GOVERNMENT ELECTIONS
Thursday 4th May 2001
BOROUGH COUNCIL COUNT
INSTRUCTIONS TO TABLE SUPERVISORS

Before the commencement of each stage. run through the procedure with your Counting Assistants. Collect their appointments from them.

NB. There are NO parish/town council elections in Bassett, Warden or Hankfield.

1. Each Supervisor will have on his table tally cards for the verification stage (Borough & Parish - if applicable), showing the ballot boxes for the Ward; the Borough postal votes for the Ward; a Count Summary sheet (Borough only); and a Doubtful Vote sheet (Borough only). There will be a supply of baskets (candidates names/party names as appropriate, doubtful votes etc.) and other assorted equipment and stationery.

2. As soon as you receive a ballot box from the Ballot Box Co-ordinator you will:-

(a)   Announce to the agents the polling station from which the box originates;

(b)   Open the box and tip the contents onto the Counting table.

(c)   Show the box to the Agents present so that they can see that it is empty.

(d)   Place the ballot box lid under the Supervisor's table.

Verification
3. The Counting assistants should then be instructed to unfold the ballot papers, keeping them face upwards, and separate the Borough ballot papers (white) from the Town/Parish (yellow).

4.The Table Supervisors will then split the counting assistants into two teams, one to count the (white) Borough ballot papers, whilst the others verify the yellow (Town/Parish) ballot papers. All papers must be counted at this stage, even those which will obviously be rejected later. Ballot papers must be kept face upwards at all times. Each counter will count the ballot papers into bundles of 25 and secure with a paper clip, then cross them into bundles of 100 and secure with a rubber band.

5. Calculate the total number of ballot papers and write this on the tally card. (White for Borough, yellow for Parish).

6. Take your tally card to the Top Table where the number will be checked against the ballot paper account received from the polling station. If the figures agree, return to your table and place the Borough ballot papers in a mixing box provided for that purpose. The parish ballot papers should be placed in a ballot box.
NB. If the figures do not agree, the ballot papers must be recounted.

7. Repeat the above process for each ballot box allocated to your table.

8. One ballot box should be retained to store the parish (if applicable) ballot papers. (See para 9.) All other ballot boxes and lids should be returned to the Ballot Box Co-ordinator.

The Mix
9. When all the ballot boxes for your ward have been verified, there should be no ballot papers left on the table. All white ballot papers should have been placed in the mixing box and all the yellow ballot papers in the Parish Ward ballot box provided for that purpose. The label provided for the parish votes should be completed with the total number of verified votes for the Ward and signed by the DRO. *(Take care, Sawworth and Wareham's End! You have two parish wards which must be*

boxed and labelled separately.)

10. When all the ballot boxes for the Ward have been verified, the Deputy Returning Officer will mix the white Borough ballot papers together with the postal votes and return the white Borough ballot papers to the counting tables. The parish verified votes will be returned to the Ballot Box Co-ordinator for secure overnight storage.

The Count

11. The counters will then sort the white ballot papers into candidates, using one of three counting methods - labelled candidate's trays (for single vacancies) or for multiple vacancies block voting templates (where party voting occurs) or counting sheets (all other).

(See separate instructions regarding single and multiple vacancy counts).

Throughout these processes, counters will be vigilant to identify doubtful votes. These are:-

· Where the voter has voted for more candidates than there are vacancies;

· Where the official mark is absent;

· Where the voter has marked the Ballot Paper in such a manner that it is not clear for whom the vote is given;

· Where the ballot paper has not been marked;

· Where the Ballot Paper has been objected to by a Counting agent;

· Where the voter has written on the Ballot Paper or has placed a mark other than a cross or a tick.

Please note that over the years it has been accepted that a tick is an acceptable mark and any votes containing ticks will not therefore be identified as doubtful.

Any doubtful votes should be placed into the Doubtful Votes Basket for adjudication by the Deputy Returning Officer.

The Deputy Returning Officer will then return the Doubtful Vote Adjudication sheet to the Supervisor to allocate the accepted votes to the candidates, using the last counting sheet. A provisional result, including any rejected votes will then be prepared for the Verification Team who will check the count totals. When this figure has been verified, the Returning Officer will inform the candidates and agents in the Candidates and Agents area of his decision regarding the doubtful votes and will announce the provisional result.

The Returning Officer's decision on rejected votes is final and can only be overturned by an Election Petition.

A recount could be requested by the candidates/agents and will be conducted at the discretion of the Returning Officer.

After the final result has been declared, Table Supervisors should place any rejected votes in the clear plastic dockets provided (these indicate the reason for the rejection). They should then be placed in an envelope for Rejected Votes and put with the counted votes in the labelled paper sack provided.

Supervisors should note the time their table duties finished and no-one should be allowed to leave without the DRO's consent, as staff may be asked to assist in the counting of votes with another table or with the general clearing up of the hall/laying out of the hall for the parish count the next morning commencing at 9.30am.

In addition to the above instructions to the Table Supervisors, some councils also issue instructions to: Each of the counting assistants, using a separate format where there is one vacancy or where there are multiple vacancies. They may also issue an overview of the verification proceedings and General instructions for the count.

For each type of count there may be separate instructions, whether the election is for parliamentary, European Parliament, local council or parish.

7

ELECTION EXPENSES

Candidates' personal expenses

As far as purely personal expenses of the candidate, such as travel and hotel costs in connection with an election, the limit that a parliamentary candidate can spend is £600 for the constituency. Any excess has to be paid by the election agent. The candidate should send a statement of such expenses to the election agent within fourteen days after the result of the election is declared.

The personal expenses of the candidate, although notified to the election agent, should not be included in the return of election expenses. For a European Parliamentary candidate in a regional election it is £900 for the region.

Maximum expenses allowable

The maximum expenses as set out in the Representation of the People Act, for each candidate, is as follows:

(a) For a parliamentary general election in a county constituency: £4,965, plus 5.6 pence for every entry in the register of electors.
For an electorate of 50,000 this would be calculated as: £4,965 plus 0.056 x 50,000 being £2,800 giving a total of £7,765

(b) For a parliamentary general election in a borough constituency: £4965, plus 4.2 pence for every entry in the register of electors.
For an electorate of 50,000 this would be calculated as:£4,965 plus the sum of 0.042 x 50,000 being £2,100 giving a total of £7,065

(c) For a parliamentary by-election in a county constituency:

£19,863, plus 22.2 pence for every entry in the register of electors.

(d) For a parliamentary by-election in a borough constituency: £19,863, plus 16.9 pence for every entry in the register of electors.

(e) For a European Parliamentary Election
The maximum amount for a registered political party is £45,000 multiplied by the number of MEP's for each electoral region.

(f) For a European Parliamentary constituency which is coterminous with a parliamentary county constituency: £5229 plus 5.9p for every entry in the register of electors.

(g) For a European Parliamentary constituency which is coterminous with a parliamentary borough constituency: £5229 plus 4.4p for every entry in the register of electors.

(h) For a by election in a European Parliamentary constituency which is coterminous with a parliamentary county constituency: £20,920 plus 23.4p for every entry in the register of electors.

(i) For a by election in a European Parliamentary constituency which is coterminous with a parliamentary borough constituency: £20,920 plus 17.8p for every entry in the register of electors.

(j) For a local government election: £219, plus 4.3 pence for every entry in the register of electors. The calculation for a ward with an electorate of 6500 would be £219 plus 0.043 x 6500 = £498.50.

(k) For a parish election. £219, plus 4.3 pence for every entry in the register of electors. The calculation for a parish ward with an electorate of 2500 would be £219 plus 0.043 x 2500 = £326.50.

Where there are two joint candidates for parish or local government elections, their maximum is reduced by one-fourth; where there are more than two, by one-third.
(Joint candidates are candidates for the same ward who employ the same election agent, clerks or messengers, or hire or use the same committee rooms, or publish joint election address or circular.)

The above rates were fixed by the Representation of the People Act 1983 as amended by later Acts.

When calculating expenses, any reference to the register of electors includes all entries, even the under age voters not yet qualified to vote. Expenses limits increase from time to time, in line with inflation. Election officers will be able to provide up to date details, usually in the form of a candidate's guide.

Where the amount exceeds £20, a bill detailing the particulars of the expense and a receipt must vouch for the expenditure. Election expenses due to be paid must be sent to the election agent within twenty-one days after the declaration of the result of the election.

It is illegal to pay any accounts which come in after that time and all election expenses must be paid within twenty-eight days after declaration of the result of the election. If paid after that time the agent is guilty of an illegal practice. Where there are disputed or late claims, the candidate, his agent or the claimant may apply to the High Court or to a county court for leave for the account to be paid.

Calculation of allowed expenses

The returning officer will issue to the candidate or agent a summary of the electorate, which will enable the correct expenses sum to be calculated. The allowed amount of expense does not include personal expenses of the candidate.

It should be noted that neither the returning officer nor his staff should be expected to work out the calculation of expenses for any candidate or election agent. The most that can be expected of the returning officer is for him to provide the means of allowing them to do it for themselves.

8

POLLING AGENTS

Definition of a polling agent

Polling agents are people sometimes appointed by the political parties to attend the polling stations to ensure that voting goes smoothly. Polling agents have to carry a card or letter issued by the returning officer, which will allow them to enter the polling station. These are the only people (apart from the electorate, the candidate and the election agent or others permitted by the returning officer) who should be allowed into a polling station.

Duties of a polling agent

A polling agent is required to read the requirement of secrecy and to help to maintain the secrecy of the ballot. In earlier times polling agents were particularly alert for people who tried to vote in another's name but this practice is now rare and if it does occur, is difficult to detect.

The agent may mark a list of the people who have voted at the election but it is an offence for him to take the marked copy away when leaving the polling station.

If a polling agent sees anything that he thinks is not correct, he should bring it to the attention of the presiding officer at the station. He can, particularly in the case of someone trying to vote in another person's name, request that the presiding officer question the voter by asking the relevant questions as required under the Regulations.

He may also request that the presiding officer arrest anyone he believes to be guilty of an offence. If he seeks this drastic remedy he must, of course, be ready to substantiate the charge in a court. The arrest can only take place before the elector leaves the polling station. The presiding officer may order a police officer to make the arrest. The word of the presiding officer is sufficient authority for the police officer to do so. However the elector should not be prevented from voting in the polling station.

Appointment of polling agents

There is no limit set on the number of polling agents that may be appointed but the candidate is responsible for the actions of any agents. They may be paid or unpaid.

If paid they must be appointed by the election agent. If unpaid, they may be appointed by the candidate himself. The candidate or the election agent should instruct polling agents about their duties.

9

COUNTING AGENTS

Definition of a counting agent

A counting agent is appointed by a candidate to oversee the the counting of the votes. He may be anyone the candidate chooses. A relative or friend will suffice but a councillor or former councillor willing to be appointed would generally speaking be ideal. All counting agents must carry a card or a letter authorising their access to the counting room.

Counting agents' duties

The counting agent's job is to ensure that the correct votes are allotted to his candidate and that the count is correctly conducted. If he is not happy with anything he should bring it to the attention of the returning officer.

Restrictions on a counting agent

Counting agents should do all in their power to ensure that the count is fair. They should not, however, handle any ballot paper or the equipment of the count, nor should they in any way impede the counters in their duties by leaning over them or distracting them.

Appointment of a counting agent

The election agent on behalf of the candidate usually arranges the appointment of counting agents. They are restricted in numbers by a statutory calculation, which is to prevent too many people impeding the proper conduct of the count.

Advice for election agents appointing counting agents

It should be borne in mind that the election staff have limited time to spare when preparing for an election and will be assisted by agents sending or taking in appointments of election agents as early as possible. This will enable the appointments to be confirmed and admission cards posted well before Election Day. Often notifications of appointments arrive at the office of election staff so near to the closing day that there is little time to process them all.

10

THE SECRECY OF THE BALLOT

Secret ballot

It is the duty of everyone attending any election, whether candidate, agent, returning officer or whoever, to help maintain the secrecy of the election, to read the requirement of secrecy and not do anything which may contravene any of the various Acts concerning the conduct of elections. There are serious penalties for contravention of any of the requirements of secrecy, which can be a fine of not more than level 5 on the statutory scale or even a prison term of up to two years.

Secret mark

A ballot paper is marked in such a way that it can be identified as either a postal vote or vote at a polling station. This mark, made by perforating the paper in a distinctive way, is part of the secrecy and security of voting.

The same pattern of perforations cannot be used again for the same type of local government election for five years or seven years for a parliamentary election. A record is kept of all such perforation marks used and this is checked for each type of election and someone will be appointed to reset all the stamping instruments to the new mark for an election.

Opening of polling station

At the opening of the polling station on election day the presiding officer has to show the empty ballot box to anybody present, if any. (It may even be his poll clerk) before he signs the label and seals the box in the prescribed manner.

In some cases where the boxes are of the metal type, the box will be sealed with tape and sealing wax together with a padlock. Where the ballot box is of the plastic type no locks are required, the boxes being secured by security pegs provided. With the plastic type of ballot box, one security peg is reserved for the end of the poll when it is used to secure the sliding portion of the box which covers the ballot paper entry slot.

Number on counterfoil

Sometimes an elector may argue that the election is not secret because his elector's number is put on the ballot paper counterfoil. He may feel this reveals how he has voted. But the ballot papers and the counterfoils are wrapped in separate packages, sealed at the end of the day and are never put together.

This of course prevents anyone tracing how a vote was cast from the number on the counterfoil. The only time that ballot papers and counterfoils could be examined together is pursuant to a court order. This would be done in strict secrecy with only the court officials having access to the papers. The need for this is to prevent abuse of the system by people who may try to vote twice or commit any manner of other offences.

After a local election the sealed packages are kept for six months only before they are destroyed. Parliamentary ballot papers are nominally delivered to the Secretary of State and are stored for five years.

11

ELECTION PETITIONS

Petitions arising out of parliamentary and local government elections

In accordance with Part III of the Representation of the People Act 1983, an election can only be challenged by a petition (brought by a petitioner - that is, anyone who voted, had a right to vote, was a candidate at the election or claiming to have the right to be elected) in a form prescribed by Rules of Court. Except for such a petition, no election can validly be questioned.

A local government election may be questioned on the grounds that the candidate whose election is challenged was at the time of the election disqualified, or was not duly elected, or on the grounds that the election was void because of corrupt or illegal practices.

A parliamentary election can only be challenged on the grounds of illegal election or non-return of election expenses within the required 35-day period.

For local government elections the 35-day period also applies but for a European Parliamentary Election there is a 50-day period for an individual candidate or 70 days by a national party agent.

The respondent to the petition

If it is the candidate who is challenged in the petition he will be the respondent to the petition. If however, the complaint is about the returning officer for a non-return of election expenses, then both he and the candidate are the respondents.

In a case involving an election in the City of London it was held that "a petition is not competent for the purpose of obtaining relief whose effect would be to unseat an elected candidate unless the candidate in question has been made a respondent" (Absalom v. Gillett 1995).

Presentation of an election petition

An election petition must be presented within 21 days after the day on which the result of the election was declared. It must be filed with, and three copies left at, the office of the Queen's Bench Masters' Secretary's Department at the Central Office of the Royal Courts of Justice, The Strand, London WC2.

Security for the costs of a petition

The petitioner must give security for all costs involved up to £5,000 or for such sum as the High Court may direct. This must be done at the time of presenting the petition or within the following three days.

Trial of the election petition

Although the statute does not directly prescribe the grounds for an election petition, certain matters in the statute constitute grounds for presenting a petition. Statutory grounds are those most frequently made use of in petitions but are by no means limited only to the statute. They can also be brought on common law grounds.

The petition must be tried in open court by a High Court judge sitting alone. For example, where there have been irregularities at the election, the election may be set aside, not withstanding that it has been conducted substantially in accordance with the law, if the result has been affected (Morgan v. Simpson 1975). Or where a returning officer improperly refused to include a candidate as being nominated.

In one instance (Gunn v. Sharpe) roughly half of the ballot papers issued at a particular polling station were not marked with the official mark. Had they been marked and counted, the result of the election would have been different.

Lord Denning stated subsequently that "Although in (Gunn v. Sharpe) the court had stated that the election was not so conducted as to be substantially in accordance with the law as to elections, the decision should have been based on the ground that the mistakes affected the result."

The courts will at times be generous in disregarding some irregularities, when it is clear that the result of the poll was not affected.

House of Commons Disqualification Act 1975

In the case of someone disqualified under the House of Commons Disqualification Act 1975, a candidate can be unseated without a petition against him. Anyone can bring this about and it is not restricted simply to those who are able to bring election petitions. Neither does it have to be carried out within the time required for bringing an election petition. It can also have effect after the time has expired for bringing an election petition.

12

THE REGISTER OF ELECTORS

Publication of Register of Electors

Each year the electoral registration officer is required to publish the register of electors. A copy of this must be available for inspection in his office and parts of the register for each electoral area have to be published in suitable public places in each area, such as sub-post offices and libraries etc. The register will remain in force until the publication of the next register.

Dates of publication

The Representation of the People Act 2000 states that the canvas for any year shall be conducted by reference to residence on the 15th of October in that year and that following the conclusion of the canvas, the register will be published on the 1st of December.

The registration officer may publish a revised version of his register at any time between the time when the register was last published and the time when it is due to be published next. He must ensure that the electoral numbers run consecutive for each part of the register and must publish a notice of his intention to publish a new register.

Alterations of registers pending elections

An alteration made in a register of electors on or after the last day for receipt of nomination papers has no effect for the purposes of that election.

Supply of computer data and labels

Computer data on disk or tape can be supplied to candidates, their agents or to political parties for use in the election of their candidate or candidates free of charge.

The right to register as an elector

The citizenship qualification

Everyone who is a citizen of the United Kingdom, citizen of the Commonwealth, or a citizen of the Republic of Ireland who is 18 years of age during the currency of the register of electors, has the right to be registered and to vote in any elections.

European citizens can vote at local and European elections only: the latter, providing they have signed an application to vote in the UK and not in their own country.

Qualifying date

Electors must register for the address at which they were living on the 15th October in the relevant year and will be eligible to be included in the register to be published the following 1st December.

Declarations of local connection for inclusion in the register

After the register of electors has been published, anybody wishing to be included must complete a form of declaration of local connection, which will enable his name and address to be included in the next register of electors.

LIST OF COMMONWEALTH COUNTRIES AS AT AUGUST 1995

HM The Queen's Realms

1. Antigua and Barbuda
2. Australia
3. The Bahamas
4. Barbados
5. Belize
6. Britain
7. Canada.
8. Grenada
9. Jamaica
10. New Zealand
11. Papua New Guinea
12. Saint Christopher & Nevis
13. St. Lucia
14. Saint Vincent & The Grenadines
15. Solomon Islands
16. Tuvulu

Indigenous Monarchies

1. Brunei
2. Lesotho
3. Malaysia
4. Swaziland
5. Tonga

Republics

1.	Bangladesh	16.	Nauru
2.	Botswana	17.	Nigeria
3.	Cyprus	18.	Pakistan
4.	Dominica	19.	Seychelles
5.	The Gambia	20.	Sierra Leone
6.	Ghana	21.	Singapore
7.	Guyana	22.	South Africa
8.	India	23.	Sri Lanka
9.	Kenya	24.	Tanzania
10.	Kiribati	25.	Trinidad and Tobago
11.	Malawi	26.	Uganda
12.	Maldives	27.	Vanunu
13.	Malta	28.	Western Samoa
14.	Mauritius	29.	Zambia
15.	Namibia	30.	Zimbabwe

Member countries of EEC (other than UK and Ireland)
Austria, Belgium, Denmark, Finland, France, Germany, Greece, Italy, Luxembourg, Netherlands, Portugal, Spain and Sweden.

Dealing with those reluctant to register

Everyone has the right to vote but this is only true if that person's name and address is recorded on the register of electors. For various reasons many people avoid putting their names on the register, and when the time comes to vote they are naturally disappointed.

The responsibility of voters to be on the electoral register does not lie with the registration officer - it lies with the voter himself. Non-registration means disenfranchisement or in other words "no vote". However, more people nowadays do appreciate the need to be on the electoral register. Loan and credit companies check the electoral register for credit references so, apart from the election benefits, there are other incentives to persuade people to be registered.

A register is produced on the 1st December every year and will include the details of everyone who has returned a registration form. If at that stage someone finds that they are not registered, this is the time to be added to the next main register.

13

CANVASSING FOR THE REGISTER

The first canvass

Each year registration forms are delivered by hand to every household in the electoral area. The initial delivery typically produces less than a 60% response so canvassing - the next stage of the process - has to be undertaken.

Canvassing on behalf of the registration officer takes place during the compilation stage of the register of electors. The canvassers then take form A with them on the follow-up stage. After the completion of this stage the canvassers again set to work on the remainders. This stage is the first canvass.

Recruiting canvassers

Canvassers are sought, sometimes from a list of previous employees and others via the Job Centre. The ideal canvasser is someone who is retired or of independent means and hence interested in work as a diversion, rather than as a means of financial support. Canvassers must also be prepared to work at effective times of day, usually in the evenings and ideally be experienced in door-to-door work or in dealing with people.

Few people will present with this profile, however, so a compromise will be necessary. Careful questioning will reveal good and bad attributes, the type of work experience applicants have and their motivation for seeking work. If the applicant is currently unemployed but still of employable age, question the adequacy of pay and whether they will have a continuing commitment. If they are in full-time employment, question their willingness to work evenings. Questioners should bear in mind the canvassers' willingness to work in difficult areas after dark as this inevitably will be a feature of their work.

How canvassers should operate

The door-to-door chasing of non-responding households is divided into two distinct stages. The first stage is the initial the follow-up, during which reminder A forms are used. These forms are identical to the original forms previously hand delivered to every household. Any changes are noted on the original or reminder form.

Canvas sheets, which list the non-responding households, are similar for each stage but need to be ruled up and filled in differently by the canvasser. Flats and bed-sits in the same building or block are treated as separate properties.

As the canvassers visit households they are asked to make an entry for each property on the canvas sheet. A property would only be considered fully dealt with if one of the following entries was obtained:

As per entry on the current register (APR)

APR plus additions (Additions refer to a new entry)

New tenants or occupiers

Foreign nationals (i.e. are not UK, British Commonwealth, Irish or European citizens)

The number of European citizens should be noted on the back of the A form in the box provided and a note made on the canvas sheet accordingly. If an answer cannot be obtained after at least two visits, the reminder form and a return envelope is put through the letterbox and the canvas sheet endorsed accordingly.

At a later stage in the canvas the canvasser will be given a letter to post through the letter box of non-responding households. He should mark on the canvas sheet the time and date he started each road.

Canvassers should report in at least once every two weeks, preferably in person. Completed canvas sheets should be handed in complete with the appropriate A forms. A telephone number should be available to canvassers if they require help.

Canvassers' work should be confined primarily to the effective hours. If there are say 20,000 non-responding households after the initial delivery (the rest having been returned by post) these will generally be the households whose members are more difficult to contact. They may simply not be interested.

Students or temporary residents in bed-sits may not even have received an A form. Some non-responders will be away on business or holiday or be elderly and cautious of doorstep callers and afraid of filling forms. The over-seventies can be identified by a marker on the canvas sheet.

Students have short term times. They can often be identified on the sheets by groups of three or more different surnames at the same property. With this in mind, between 5.30 pm and 8 pm is the best time, this being when workers and students generally arrive home and before they go out again. Later than 9 pm is not recommended.

Weekends are also good but early calls - particularly on Sunday before 10.30 am - are likely to annoy those hoping for a lie-in. Earlier daytime calls will be fairly unresponsive, particularly in bed-sit areas University Christmas term times start around 4th October and finish around 10th December. The Easter term might be from 15th January to 3rd April and the summer term from 28th April to 30th June.

Signatures must be obtained where at all possible on A forms or later on canvas sheets. The elector's own signature is preferable but another in the house will be acceptable. Neighbours can usually be asked to help, providing canvassers make it clear who they are by producing their identity cards.

Sometimes neighbours know only the first names but even these may help as evidence. Neighbours may also be persuaded to sign forms if it is explained they are only confirming information. It may be difficult though to obtain detailed information such as dates of occupancy and the birthdays of rising 18 year olds in this way.

Bed-sits in old houses are likely to be the hardest properties of all to canvas. Obtaining access at all may be difficult and identifying room numbers sometimes almost impossible. All the canvasser can do is work from canvas sheets for existing occupants and where in doubt, get as many names or claim forms from those not named even if they cannot be identified against particular rooms.

Some tips for canvassers

The following guidance was given to canvassers in Reading during my term of office.

1. Plan your walk carefully in advance. Arrange "A" forms and canvasser sheets in the same order. Carry a clipboard if you can.

2. Always carry a torch, even during the day, as some multiple occupancy properties are very dark inside. Also carry at least two working pens.

3. At the doorstep do not hand over forms for electors to fill in. Do this yourself showing the form to the elector. Do not let him search for original forms or evidence of identity. All of this wastes time and your job is to accept what you are told.

4. Always check that there are no other eligible people at the property, particularly 16/17 year olds. Ask this as you are completing the form.

5. Do not get into arguments or discussions, particularly political. If the resident refuses to give information, even after gentle persuasion, accept this and mark canvas sheet accordingly.

6. Ask next door (but no further away) if there is no response from a household. As you are completing the forms check if next door is also on the canvas sheet. If it is, ask if residents can confirm names of neighbours. This will save time if the residents next door prove to be out.

7. Try to avoid entering houses at all unless this is necessary to find flats or bed-sits. It only wastes time and your torch will deal with poor lighting at the doorstep.

8. For the sake of your sanity, remove elastic bands from canvas sheets and envelopes before you start!

Answers to questions canvassers are likely to encounter

The questions below are ones that canvassers frequently report being asked:

Q. Why should I register when I don't want to vote?
A. All qualifying citizens are required to register under the

Representation of the People Act 1949. There is a heavy penalty for refusing to register, currently a fine of up to £1000. In practice it is rarely imposed. (but don't tell a recalcitrant elector that!)

Q. Why does the Council want this information?
A. Only to compile the register of electors. It is however, a public document and can be examined by anyone.

Q. Can my name be put on an anonymous part of the register?
A.You can put your name on a register that is not sold but it will appear on any register used for elections.

Q. Apart from my right to vote, what other advantages are there to being on the register?
A. The principal one is the ability to obtain credit, a mortgage or open a bank account. Credit houses routinely scrutinise the registers to establish that applicants have a fixed address.

Q. Won't mailing houses use the lists for names and address?
A. Yes, although they tend to want more detailed information such as leisure interests, credit rating, nationality, and age. This type of information is not available from the register of electors.

Q. Why do they want to know if I am over seventy?
A. Only to place you on an unpublished list of people not liable for jury service.

Q. I am too ill/old to get to the polling station/will be abroad on business/ will be away on holiday on the day of the election. Can I vote by post or proxy?
A. It is possible. You will be sent an application form. (This also applies to people who have moved to a new address after the 15th October, providing they are registered at their old

address for that date)

Q. Is this anything to do with council tax?
A. No. The council tax is levied from a completely separate source.

Q. I am the householder or head of house. Why is my name not on the top of the list in the register of electors?
A. The register of electors is compiled in alphabetical order to enable you to obtain your vote at the polling station with the minimum of delay.

14

ASSISTANCE FOR DISABLED PERSONS and POSTAL AND PROXY VOTES

Assistance for people with disabilities.

Each polling station has at least one large version of the ballot paper to assist voters who are partially sighted. There will be a device prescribed for enabling blind or partially sighted voters to vote unaided.

The device is likely to be in the form of a template. The template will have holes, which correspond with the spaces for candidates. The holes will be large enough for the elector to mark the paper through the hole. A voter disabled by blindness, physical incapacity or the inability to read, can make a request verbally or in writing to a presiding officer at the polling station, for a companion to assist them to vote.

Postal or Proxies for people with disabilities.

Anyone who is entered on the register of electors has a right to vote by post if they cannot reasonably be expected to go to their allotted polling station because of a disability, either physical or sensory. They can apply by using a postal or proxy vote form.

The previous complex system of postal voting meant the storage and handling of many different forms. The Representation of the People Act 2000 has simplified the situation, and there should now only be a need for one type of form. The same form will cover postal and proxy for all elections.

People in business

Anybody who is going to be away from the area of their polling station on business at the time of any election, is entitled to a vote either by post or proxy. (A proxy is someone who will be willing to go to the polling station for them and cast their vote in the ballot box).

Should the proxy be a postal voter in his own right or live in another area or borough, too far to travel then the proxy may apply for a vote by post for the elector they are acting for. This is called a postal proxy.

The application for a post or proxy vote is out for either an indefinite or a fixed period. It remains in force unless cancelled or amended by the elector in the meantime. Should the elector move to another address within the borough while the postal vote is still active, the vote can be redirected to the new address. If he moves out of the borough while the vote is still active, it can be redirected only during the currency of the register and would cease when the elector is no longer registered.

It should be noted however, that the timetable or notice of election should be checked for closing dates of postal or proxy vote applications. Visit or call the registration office if unsure that an application for a postal or proxy vote has been accepted or to make a new application.

Candidates or election agents are allowed to have a quantity of postal voting application forms for distribution on their rounds of the electorate.

Overseas electors

Many British citizens living abroad have the right to vote at parliamentary and European parliamentary elections held in the UK (this does not include local government elections). To vote they must register as an overseas elector.

To qualify they must:
a) make an application on the relevant date, ("the relevant date" means the date they completed the application)

b) be a British citizen and not subject to any legal incapacity to vote and not living within any address in the UK

c) have been living in the constituency concerned, on the qualifying date for that register and no more than twenty years should have passed before the date of their application to register as an overseas elector

(If they were too young to be on the electoral register based on the last qualifying date before they left the country, a parent or guardian's inclusion in the electoral register on the relevant

date and for the relevant address will suffice.)

The registration must be renewed each period of 12 months from the date of any application.

Only British citizens can register as overseas electors. Other Commonwealth citizens or citizens of the Republic of Ireland can register and vote at UK elections only when resident in the UK.

Anyone can get a registration form (by writing or in person) from the British consular or diplomatic mission. They will need to give their full name and overseas address; the UK address where they were last registered (or the address where they were living on the last qualifying date before they left the country), and the date they left the UK.

If this is the first time they have made an overseas elector's declaration (or if they have been registered as an elector living in the UK since making the previous declaration) they will have to give additional information to show British citizenship.

If they left the UK before they were old enough to register, they will have to provide a copy of their full birth certificate and information about the parent or guardian whose registration they are relying on.

If this is the first time they have made an overseas declaration, they will have to find someone to support what they say in their declaration. This can be anyone who is aged 18 years or over; has a British passport, which describes his or her status as a British citizen; is not living in the UK and knows the applicant but is not a close relative (husband, wife, parent, grandparent, brother, sister, child or grandchild). Someone living in the UK cannot support this type of application.

Each year when anyone is registered as an overseas elector, the registration officer will send him or her a reminder for the following year. They must complete and return this form as soon as possible so that their registration can continue. Reminders are as a rule sent out in June or July.

15

THE ARMED FORCES

Registration of service personnel

Servicemen and women can register using a service registration card but they can, if they meet the requirements of residence, have the additional option to register the same as any other voter, at their home address or as overseas electors.

Postal and proxy votes for service personnel

Some service voters appoint a proxy to act for them at election time, while others vote by post. Should the proxy be unable to go to the polling station, they can obtain a postal proxy vote, for which they make the application themselves.

Registration index

The Army, Navy and Air Force services registrations are controlled by the following offices:

Army: Army Electoral Registration Index
Higher Barracks, Exeter EX4 4ND.
Tel: 01392 492171

Navy: Royal Naval Registration Index
H.M.S. Centurion,
Grange Road,
Gosport, PO13 9XA.
Tel: 01705 22351

RAF: RAF Electoral Registration Index,
RAF Personnel Management Centre,
Royal Air Force, Innsworth,
Gloucester, GL3 1EZ.
Tel: 01452 712612

From time to time registration cards are sent to the wrong authority. Service registration officers are often not sure where the boundaries are for the parliamentary constituencies. These should be forwarded by the registration officer to the correct council with the minimum delay.

16

THE DATA PROTECTION ACT 1984 and 1998 and Junk Mail

The introduction of the Act

The Data Protection Act received Royal Assent on 12 July 1984 and has been updated by the Act of 1998. Electoral registration officers who use computers in compiling the register of electors are subject to and likely to be affected by some of its provisions. Similarly affected may be political parties who keep computerised records of canvassing returns.

Data users

Under the Act, people who use and control the contents and use of automatically processed personal data are classed as data users and must register with the data protection registrar. However, this obligation does not apply in relation to any data, which is required by law to be made available to the public.

In order to comply with the principals of data protection and the EU Data Protection Directive, the public should be informed as to the uses that the register of electors might be put. The public can request that their names and details are not included in a register of electors which is offered for sale. Names and addresses of those who opt out will only be included in an edited version of the register which will be available for voting purposes only.

Non-public information

The parts of the electoral database which holds information regarding who is over seventy and military service personnel records are not part of the published register and are therefore subject to the Act and need to be registered.

Purchase of data

Computer data on disk or tape can be supplied to anyone on payment of a prescribed fee. In data form, the fee will be £1 for each 1000 entries in the register or part of a 1000. In printed form, and that does not mean the printed register, the fee will be £3 for each 1000 entries or part of 1000.

Overseas electors lists can also be purchased, the fee being £5 in data form plus £1 for each hundred entries over 100 and in printed form £5 plus £3 for each hundred entries over 100 or part of 100. This would applies only to the published register; all other data is extracted beforehand. Members of Parliament, candidates, and their electoral agents are allowed to have the data free of charge providing it is for use in connection with an election.

The effect of the Act on political parties

Political parties which hold computerised information derived from the electoral register need to register under the Act. This applies despite the fact that the information they will be able to obtain has had the non-public parts removed. Anyone is entitled to ask a political party, as a data holder, to disclose what information it holds on him. The party is entitled to charge £10 for providing this.

"Junk Mail"and the Electoral Register

Unsolicited mail, often called "junk mail", causes some people a lot of annoyance and is often blamed on the electoral register. Some of it can be prevented by those so inclined.

The electoral register is not in fact always the cause of the problem. Businesses from whom a person they may have purchased something in the past often keep the address on file and sometimes use these lists to promote a product by sending out leaflets. This can be stopped by writing to the business asking for the complainant's name to be excluded from any further mailing lists.

To prevent unsolicited mail from businesses they have never dealt with and do not want information from members of the public contact the Mailing Preference Service. This is a service available from the Post Office. Upon request a Freepost application form will be sent to anyone wishing to stop unsolicited mail shots. The unwanted mail will not stop immediately but will eventually reduce if not stop altogether.

The address of this service is: The Mailing Preference Service, Freepost, London W1E 7EZ.

17

PARISH AND COMMUNITY ELECTIONS

Parish and local government elections

Parish and community elections are very similar to local government elections and in some boroughs, where there are parish or community councils, these would normally be combined with the local elections. There are many minor differences in the two types of election. For instance there is no requirement for an election agent to be appointed in parish and community elections. (see notes below)

The form of nomination is the same as that used in local elections but it only has to be subscribed to by two electors for the electoral area as proposer and seconder. No other assentors are required.

The procedure for parish and community elections

The expression electoral area in the case of a parish or community election means the parish or community itself. If however the parish or community is divided into electoral wards the electoral area means a ward.

The Parishes and Communities Rules define the electoral number as the distinctive letter or letters of the parliamentary polling district into which the parish falls and the distinctive electors number as printed in the register of electors. It is these numbers and letters, which are entered on the nomination paper: a wrong number used could invalidate the paper.

Postal voting is now allowed at all elections. The returning officer is required to send to each postal voter a ballot paper; a declaration of identity marked with the ballot paper number and the colour of the ballot paper; an envelope for their return (the covering envelope); and a smaller envelope marked 'ballot paper envelope' bearing the number of the ballot paper.

At parish or community elections anybody who is appointed by the candidate may attend the issuing of the postal votes.

Casual Vacancies

1. A casual vacancy for a parish councillor must be filled by an election only if a request for an election is given to the Returning Officer of a district council in which the parish is situated, signed by ten local government electors for the electoral area, within a period of fourteen days (computed), commencing on the day after public notice of the vacancy has been given.

2. If no request for an election is received within the timescale the parish council must fill the vacancy by co-option.

3. If a request is duly received, an election must be held to fill the vacancy and the parish council cannot co-opt, irrespective of whether there are sufficient nominations.

4. If a request for an election is duly received, the election shall be held within sixty days (computed) commencing on the day when public notice of the vacancy was given.

5. A nomination paper must include the signatures of a proposer and seconder only. (Both, local government electors for the parish [ward]).

6. The consent to nomination includes an added residency qualification that the candidate must live within 4.8 kilometres of the parish.

7. In an uncontested election, the returning officer shall as soon as practicable after the last time for delivery of notices of withdrawals of candidature:-
a) Declare to be elected the person(s) remaining validly nominated
b) Give notice of the name of each such person to the proper officer of the parish council, or, if there is no proper officer, to the chairman of the council or if there is no chairman, to the proper officer of the district in which the parish is situate

c) Give public notice of the name of each such person

8. In an uncontested election, the returning officer shall send to each newly elected councillor a Notice to persons Elected advising of the statutory requirement (Section 83 of the Local Government Act 1972) to make a declaration of acceptance of Office (see paragraph 13 of these notes).

9. A candidate at an election of parish councillors need not have an election agent.

10. The Notice of Election must be published in the electoral area (i.e. In the relevant parish/ward) and at the offices of the district/borough council.

11. Not later than noon on the nineteenth day before the election a parish council may request poll cards to be printed at their expense.

12. The declaration of acceptance of a parish councillor must be made before or at the first meeting after election. After that, the declaration can only be made if alternative arrangements have been approved at the first meeting after election.
If the declaration is not made then, or if the alternative arrangements are not approved at the first meeting after election, it appears that there is no way in which a declaration can be lawfully be made.

13. Returns and declarations of candidates' election expenses must be submitted to the returning officer, within 28 days (not computed) of the declaration of result of poll.

18

COMBINED ELECTIONS

Elections which must be combined

a) The polls at a parliamentary general election must be combined with a European parliamentary election if they are held on the same day

b) An ordinary local government election must be combined with a parliamentary general election if they are held on the same day

c) An ordinary local government election must be combined with a European parliamentary election if they are held on the same day

Elections which may be combined

The polls at other European, parliamentary and local government elections may be combined if they occur in areas which come within the same boundary or are situated wholly or partly within each other, and the returning officer for each election considers it practicable to combine them. The polls are said to be combined if the same polling stations are used for more than one election.

The voters are issued with ballot papers for each election, which means that the same polling staff would be used, therefore reducing the overall cost of the elections. Any costs incurred would be split between the elections except where they can be attributed to one election in particular.

Returning Officers at Combined Elections

At combined elections one officer should assume responsibility for both elections. It would fall on the returning officer for a parliamentary constituency if one of the elections were for a European parliament. It would never be the returning officer for the European election.

Ballot papers and registers
Ballot papers at combined elections should have different colours, which clearly distinguish them from each other. The registers should be marked in a different colour for each type of election.

Lists of disabled voters and tendered ballot papers etc.
The same lists may be used for combined elections: they only need to identify for which election the papers were issued.

Ballot Boxes
The same ballot box must be used for ballot papers of both elections.

Poll Cards
It is the responsibility of the returning officer to issue poll cards; these may be combined on the same card or issued separately.

Postal Ballot Papers
If a voter spoils one ballot paper at a combined election, he must also return any other paper issued with it before a replacement can be issued.

Timing of a Combined Election
In a European or parliamentary general election combined with any other election the times of opening of the polls will be 7. a.m. to 10. p.m.

If a parliamentary General Election is called for on the same day as the scheduled ordinary elections of district and parish councillors, the law provides for the parliamentary and district polls to be combined and the parish polling day to be postponed for three weeks.

If the election is combined with a parliamentary General Election or European parliamentary election the polling will be from 7.00 am to 10.00 pm.

A poll at a parish or community council election would normally be combined with the local government elections and held on the same day between 8.00 am and 9.00 pm. The cost of the two elections is divided between the two except for any items, which are directly attributable to one or other of the elections.

All notices in polling booths at combined polls should reflect the fact that they are combined with another election. The guidance to voters notice must provide details as to how the voter should mark the paper and how many candidates to vote for on each paper, as well as giving details of the colour of the paper and which election the paper is for.

19

REPRESENTATION OF THE PEOPLE ACT 2000

This chapter contains Part I of the Representation of the People Act 2000 in full, and a summary of the remainder of the Act.

The Act introduces changes to the electoral procedures and to the electoral law, which make it easier for the disabled and others to vote. A scheme which makes the register of electors a rolling one, doing away with a single annual qualifying date for registration, will also mean more people will be able to vote.

This rolling register will mean that the homeless and mental health patients - other than those detained as a consequence of criminal activity - or prisoners on remand (but not convicted prisoners) - who might not have been qualified at the old 'single' qualifying date may well qualify under the new system. Any of these can complete a declaration of local connection, claiming that they live, or have lived, in the locality.

In order to comply with the principals of data protection and the EU Data Protection Directive, the public should be informed as to the uses that the register of electors might be put. Any member of the public can then opt out of being included in any register that is available for sale. The names and addresses of those who do opt out would still appear on any register that is required for electoral purposes and would still be available for local inspection.

Under the new Act any candidate supplying false information on a nomination paper would be committing an offence.

Pilot schemes are to be put into operation under which an authority can submit a proposal to the Secretary of State if they wish to try another method of voting, such as by some means of electronic voting or use of mobile polling stations, etc. Returning officers will assess the result of any changes they are permitted to make and will be expected to publish a report in the local area as well as send one copy of the report to the Secretary of State.

Representation of the People Act 2000

An Act to make new provisions with respect to the registration of voters for the purposes of parliamentary and local government elections; and for connected purposes.

[9th March 2000]

BE IT ENACTED by the Queen's most Excellent Majesty, by and with the advice and consent of the Lords Spiritual and Temporal, and Commons, in this present Parliament assembled, and by the authority of the same, as follows:-

Part I

ELECTORAL REGISTRATION AND FRANCHISE

New system of registration

New system of electoral Registration.

1. - (1) For sections 1 and 2 of the Representation of the People Act 1983 ("the 1983 Act") there shall be substituted-

"Parliamentary electors

1. - (1) A person is entitled to vote as an elector at a parliamentary election in any constituency if on the date of the poll he-

(a) is registered in the register of parliamentary electors for that constituency;

(b) is not subject to any legal incapacity to vote (age apart);

(c) is either a Commonwealth citizen or a citizen of the Republic of Ireland; and

(d) is of voting age (that is, 18 years or over).

(2) A person is not entitled to vote as an elector-

(a) more than once in the same constituency at any parliamentary election; or

(b) in more than one constituency at a general election.

Local government electors

2.- (1) A person is entitled to vote as an elector at a local government election in any electoral area if on the date of poll he-

(a) is registered in the register of local government electors for

65

that area;

(b) is not subject to any legal incapacity to vote (age apart);

(c) is a Commonwealth citizen, a citizen of the Republic of Ireland or a relevant citizen of the Union; and

is of voting age (that is, 18 years or over)

(2) A person is not entitled to vote as an elector -

(a) more than once in the same electoral area at any local government election; or

(b) in more than one electoral area at an ordinary election for a local government area which is not a single electoral area."

(2) For section 4 of the 1983 Act there shall be substituted-

"Entitlement to registration

Entitlement to be registered as parliamentary or local government elector.

4. (1) A person is entitled to be registered in the register of parliamentary electors for any constituency or part of a constituency if on the relevant date he -

(a) is resident in the constituency or that part of it;

(b) is not subject to any legal incapacity to vote (age apart);

(c) is either a qualifying Commonwealth citizen or a citizen of the Republic of Ireland; and

(d) is of voting age.

(2) A person is not entitled to be registered in the register of parliamentary electors for any constituency in Northern Ireland unless, in addition to complying with subsection (1) above, he has been resident in Northern Ireland during the whole of the period of three months ending on the relevant date.

(3) A person is entitled to be registered in the register of local government electors for any electoral area if on the relevant date he -

(a) is resident in that area;

(b) is not subject to any legal incapacity to vote (age apart);

(c) is a qualifying Commonwealth citizen, a citizen of the Republic of Ireland or a relevant citizen of the Union; and

(d) is of voting age.

(4) The preceding provisions have effect -

(a) subject to -

(i) any enactment imposing a disqualification for registration as a parliamentary, or (as the case may be) local government, elector; and

(ii) compliance with any prescribed requirements; and

(b) (as respects registration as a parliamentary elector) without prejudice to section 2(1) of the Representation of the People Act 1985 (registration of British citizens overseas).

(5) A person otherwise qualified is (despite subsection (1)(d) or (3)(d), as the case may be) entitled to be registered in a register of parliamentary electors or local government electors if he will attain voting age before the end of the period of 12 months beginning with the 1st December next following the relevant date, but -

(a) his entry in the register shall give the date on which he will attain that age; and

(b) until the date given in the entry he shall not by virtue of the entry be treated as an elector for any purposes other than those of an election date of the poll for which is the date so given or any later date.

(6) In this section-

"qualifying Commonwealth citizen" means a Commonwealth citizen who either -

(a) is not a person who requires leave under the Immigration Act 1971 to enter or remain in the United Kingdom, or

(b) is such a person but for the time being has (or is, by virtue of any enactment, to be treated as having) any description of such leave;

"the relevant date", in relation to a

person, means -

(a) the date on which an application for registration is made (or, by virtue of section 10A(2) below, is treated as having been made) by him;

(b) in the case of a person applying for registration in pursuance of a declaration of local connection or a service declaration, the date on which the declaration was made."

Disfranchisement

Disfranchisement of offenders detained in mental hospitals

2. After section 3 of the 1983 Act there shall be inserted-
"Disfranchisement of offenders detained in mental hospitals

3A. - (1) A person to whom this section applies is, during the time that he is-

(a) detained at any place in pursuance of the order or direction by virtue of which this section applies to him, or

(b) unlawfully at large when he would otherwise be so detained,

legally incapable of voting at any parliamentary or local government election.

(2) As respects England and Wales, this section applies to the following persons-

(a) any person in respect of whom -

(i) an order has been made under section 37, 38, 44 or 51 (5) of the Mental Health Act 1983, or

(ii) a direction has been given under section 45A, 46 or 47 of that Act;

(b) any person in respect of whom an order has been made under section 5 (2)(a) of the Criminal Procedure (Insanity) Act 1964; and

(c) any person in respect of whom the Court of Appeal has made an order under -

(i) section 6(2)(a) of the Criminal Appeal Act 1968, or

(ii) section 14(2)(a) of that Act.

(3) As respects Scotland, this section applies to the following persons -

(a) any person in respect of whom an order has been made under section 53, 54, 57(2)(a) or (b) or 58 of the Criminal Procedure (Scotland) Act 1995; and

(b) any person in respect of whom a direction has been given under section 69 of the Mental Health (Scotland) Act 1984 or section 71 of that Act (being a person to whom that section applies by virtue of subsection (2)(a) of that section or section 59A of that Act of 1995.

(4) As respects Northern Ireland, this section applies to the fol-

lowing persons-

(a) any person in respect of whom -

(i) an order has been made under Article 44, 45, 50A(2)(a) or 57(5) of the Mental Health (Northern Ireland) Order 1986, or

(ii) a direction has been given under Article 52 or 53 of that Order; and

(b) any person in respect of whom the Court of Appeal has made an order under-

(i) section 11(1)(b) or (2)(b) of the Criminal Appeal (Northern Ireland) Act 1980, or

(ii) section 13(5A) of that Act.

(5) As respects any part of the United Kingdom, this section applies to any person in respect of whom an admission order has been made under -

(a) section 116B of the Army Act 1955 or the Air Force Act 1955, or

(b) section 63B of the Naval Discipline Act 1957.

(6) In this section any reference to a person in respect of whom any order or direction falling within subsection (2), (3) or (4) has been made or given includes a reference to a person in respect of whom any such order or direction is, by virtue of any enactment, to be treated as having been made or given in connection with his transfer to a place in the part of the United Kingdom mentioned in that subsection.

(7) Any reference in any of subsections (2) to (4) above to a provision of any Act or Order includes a reference to any earlier provision (whether of that Act or Order as originally enacted or made or as previously amended, or otherwise) to the like effect."

Residence for the purposes of registration

Residence for purposes of registration: general

3. For section 5 of the 1983 Act there shall be substituted

Residence: general

5. - (1) This section applies where the question whether a person is resident at a particular address on the relevant date for the purposes of section 4 above falls to be determined for the

purposes of that section.

(2) Regard shall be had, in particular, to the purpose and other circumstances, as well as to the fact, of his presence at, or absence from, the address on that date.

For example, where at a particular time a person is staying at any place otherwise than on a permanent bases, he may in all the circumstances be taken to be at that time -

(a) resident there if he has no home elsewhere, or

(b) not resident there if he does have a home elsewhere.

(3) For the purpose of determining whether a person is resident in a dwelling on the relevant date for the purposes of section 4 above, his residence in the dwelling shall not be taken to have been interrupted by reason of his absence in the performance of any duty arising from or incidental to any office, service or employment held or undertaken by him if -

(a) he intends to resume actual residence within six months of giving up such residence, and will not be prevented from doing so by the performance of that duty; or

(b) the dwelling serves as a permanent place of residence (whether for himself or for himself and another persons) and he would be in actual residence there but for his absence in the performance of that duty.

(4) For the purposes of subsection (3) above any temporary period of unemployment shall be disregarded.

(5) Subsection (3) above shall apply in relation to a person's absence by reason of his attendance on a course provided by an educational institution as it applies in relation to a person's absence in the performance of any duty such as is mentioned in that subsection.

(6) Subject to sections 7 and 7A below, a person who is detained at any place in legal custody shall not, by reason of his presence there, be treated for the purposes of section 4 above as resident there."

Residence: patients in mental hospitals who are not detained offenders or on remand.

4. For section 7 of the 1983 Act there shall be substituted -
"Residence: patients in mental hospitals who are not detained
offenders or on remand.

7. - (1) This section applies to a person who -

(a) is a patient in a mental hospital (whether or not he is liable
to be detained there), but

(b) is not a person to whom section 3A above or section 7A
below applies.

(2) A person to whom this section applies shall (subject to subsection (5) below) be regarded for the purposes of section 4
above as resident at the mental hospital in question if the length
of the period which he is likely to spend at the hospital is sufficient for him to be regarded as being resident there for the
purposes of electoral registration.

(3) A person registered in a register of electors in pursuance of
an application for registration made by virtue of subsection (2)
above is entitled to remain registered until -

(a) the end of the period of 12 months beginning with the date
when the entry in the register first takes effect, or

(b) another entry made in respect of him in any register of electors rakes effect (whether or not in pursuance of an application
made by virtue of subsection (2)),

Whichever first occurs.

(4) Where the entitlement of such a person to remain so registered terminates by virtue of subsection (3) above, the registration officer concerned shall remove that person's entry from the
register, unless he is entitled to remain registered in pursuance
of a further application made by virtue of subsection (2).

(5) Subsection (2) above shall not be taken as precluding the
registration of a person to whom this section applies -

(a) by virtue of his residence at some place other than the mental hospital in which he is a patient, or

(b) in pursuance of a declaration of local connection.

(6) In this section "mental hospital" means any establishment
(or part of an establishment) maintained wholly or mainly for
the reception and treatment of persons suffering from any form
of mental disorder; and for this purpose "mental disorder" -

(a) in relation to England or Wales, has the same meaning as in the Mental Health Act 1983,
(b) in relation to Scotland, has the same meaning as in the Mental Health (Scotland) Act 1984, and
(c) in relation to Northern Ireland, has the same meaning as in the Mental Health (Northern Ireland) Order 1986."

Residence: persons remanded in custody etc.
5. After section 7 of the 1983 Act (as substituted by section 4 above) there shall be inserted -
"Residence: persons remanded in custody etc.
7A. - (1) This section applies to a person who is detained at any place pursuant to a relevant order or direction and is so detained otherwise than after -
(a) being convicted of any offence, or
(b) a finding in criminal proceedings that he did the act or made the omission charged.
(2) A person to whom this section applies shall (subject to sub-section (5) below) be regarded for the purposes of section 4 above as resident at the place at which he is detained if the length of the period which he is likely to spend at that place is sufficient for him to be regarded as being resident there for the purposes of electoral registration.
(3) A person registered in a register of electors in pursuance of an application for registration made by virtue of subsection (2) above is entitled to remain so registered until -
(a) the end of the period of 12 months beginning with the date when the entry in the register first takes effect, or
(b) another entry made in respect of him in any register of electors takes effect (whether or not in pursuance of an application made by virtue of subsection (2)),
Whichever first occurs.
(4) Where the entitlement of such a person to remain so registered terminates by virtue of subsection (3) above, the registration officer concerned shall remove that person's entry from the register, unless he is entitled to remain registered in pursuance of a further application made by virtue of subsection (2).

(5) Subsection (2) above shall not be taken as precluding the registration of a person to whom this section applies -
(a) by virtue of his residence at some place other than the place at which he is detained, or
(b) in pursuance of a declaration of local connection.
(6) In this section "a relevant order or direction" means -
(a) a remand or committal in custody;
(b) a remand to a hospital under section 35 or 36 of the Mental Health (Northern Ireland) Order 1986;
(c) a direction for removal to a hospital under section 48 of that Act or Article 54 of that Order;
(d) a committal to a hospital under section 52 of the Criminal Procedure (Scotland) Act 1995; or
(e) a transfer order under section 70 of the Mental Health (Scotland) Act 1984 or a transfer direction under section 71 of that Act made in respect of a person to whom that section applies by virtue of subsection (2)© of that section."

Notional residence: declarations of local connection.
6. After section 7A of the 1983 Act (as inserted by section 5 above) there shall be inserted -
"Notional residence declarations of local connection.
7B. - (1) A declaration under this section ("a declaration of local connection") -
(a) may be made only by a person to whom this section applies, but
(b) may be made by such a person despite the fact that by reason of his age he is not entitled to vote.
(2) This section applies to any person who on the date when he makes such a declaration is -
(a) a person to whom section 7 above applies and who would not be entitled to be registered by virtue of residence at any place other than the mental hospital (within the meaning of that section) at which he is a patient, or
(b) a person to whom section 7A applies and who would not be entitled to be registered by virtue of residence at any place other than the place at which he is detained as mentioned in

subsection (1) of that section, or

(c) a person who does not fall within paragraph (a) or (b) above (and is not otherwise in legal custody) and who is not, for the purposes of section 4 above, resident at any address in the United Kingdom (a "homeless person").

(3) A declaration of local connection shall state -

(a) the name of the declarant and either -

(i) an address to which correspondence for him from either the registration officer concerned or the returning officer can be delivered, or

(ii) that he is willing to collect such correspondence periodically from the registration officer's office;

(b) the date of the declaration;

(c) that on the date of the declaration the declarant falls into one of the categories of persons to whom this section applies, specifying -

(i) the category in question, and

(ii) (in the case of a person falling within subsection (2)(a) or (b) above) the name and address of the mental hospital at which he is a patient or (as the case may be) of the place at which he is detained;

(d) the required address (as defined by subsection (4) below);

(e) that on the date of the declaration the declarant is a Commonwealth citizen or a citizen of the Republic of Ireland or (if the declaration is made for the purposes only of local government elections) a relevant citizen of the Union;

(f) whether the declarant has on the date of the declaration attained the age of 18 years, and, if he has not, the date of his birth.

(4) For the purposes of this section "the required address" is -

(a) in the case of a person falling within subsection (2)(a) or (b) above -

(i) the address in the United Kingdom where he would be residing if he were not such a patient, or detained, as mentioned in that provision, or

(ii) if he cannot give such an address, an address in the United Kingdom at which he has resided;

(b) in the case of a homeless person, the address of, or which is nearest to, a place in the United Kingdom where he commonly spends a substantial part of his time (whether during the day or at night).

(5) Where a declaration of local connection is made for the purposes of registration in Northern Ireland, the declaration must state that the declarant has been in Northern Ireland during the whole of the period of three months ending on the date of the declaration.

(6) Where a declaration of local connection made by a homeless person is delivered to the registration officer concerned during the period -

(a) beginning with the date when a vacancy occurs -

(i) in the seat for the parliamentary constituency within which the required address falls, or

(ii) in the seat for any Scottish Parliament constituency or National Assembly for Wales constituency with which it falls, and

(b) ending on the final nomination day (within the meaning of section 13B below) for the parliamentary by-election, or (as the case may be) the election under section 9 of the Scotland Act 1998 or section 8 of the Government of Wales Act 1998, held in respect of that vacancy,

the declaration must state that, during the period of three months ending on the date of the declaration, the declarant has commonly been spending a substantial part of his time (whether during the day or at night) at, or near, the required address.

(7) No declaration of local connection shall be specially made by a person for the purposes of local government elections, and any such declaration made for the purposes of parliamentary elections shall have effect also for the purposes of local government elections; but -

(a) a declaration of local connection may be made for the purposes only of local government elections by a person who is as a peer subject to a legal incapacity to vote at parliamentary elections or by a relevant citizen of the Union; and

(b) where so made, shall be marked to show that it is available for local government elections only, but shall in all other respects be the same as other declarations of local connection.

(8) If a person -

(a) makes a declaration of local connection stating more than one address under subsection (3)(d) above, or

(b) makes more than one declaration of local connection bearing the same date and stating different addresses under that provision,

the declaration or declarations shall be void.

(9) A declaration of local connection may be cancelled at any time by the declarant.

(10) A declaration of local connection shall be of no effect unless it is received by the registration officer concerned within the period of three months beginning with the date of the declaration.

Effect of declaration of local connection

7C. - (1) Where a person's declaration of local connection is in force when he applies for registration, he shall be regarded for the purposes of section 4 above as -

(a) resident on the date of the declaration at the address stated in it in accordance with section 7B(3)(d) above; and

(b) for the purposes of registration in Northern Ireland, as resident in Northern Ireland during the whole of the period of three months ending with that date.

(2) A person registered in a register of electors in pursuance of a declaration of local connection is entitled to remain so registered until -

(a) the end of the period of 12 months beginning with the date when the entry in the register first takes effect,

(b) the declaration is cancelled under section 7B(9) above, or

(c) another entry made in respect of him in any register of electors takes effect (whether or not in pursuance of a declaration of local connection),

Whichever first occurs.

(3) Where the entitlement of such a person to remain so regis-

tered terminates by virtue of subsection (2) above, the registration officer concerned shall remove that person's entry from the register, unless he is entitled to remain registered in pursuance of a further declaration of local connection.

(4) This section shall not be taken as precluding the registration of a person falling within section 7B(2)(a) or (b) above in pursuance of an application made by virtue of section 7(2) or 7A(2) above."

Service voters
Service declarations.
7. Section 12(3) and (4) of the 1983 Act (by virtue of which persons with service qualifications may only be registered in pursuance of a service declaration, even where they would otherwise be entitled to be registered by virtue of residence in the United Kingdom) shall cease to have effect.

Further amendments
Further amendments about registration.
8. Schedules 1, 2 and 3, which make consequential and connected amendments of -
(a) the 1983 Act,
(b) sections 1 to 3 of the Representation of the People Act 1985 (overseas electors), and
(c) the Electoral Authorities (Northern Ireland) Act 1989,
Respectively, shall have effect.

Supply of information contained in register
Restriction on supply of information contained in register.
9. - (1) Schedule 2 to the 1983 Act (provisions which may be contained in regulations as to registration) is amended as follows.

(2) For paragraphs 10 and 11 there shall be substituted -
"10. - (1) Provisions requiring a registration officer to prepare, in addition to the version of the register which he is required to prepare by virtue of the other provisions of this Act ("the full

register"), a version of the register which omits the names and addresses of registered electors by or on behalf of whom requests have been made to have their names and addresses excluded from that version of it ("the edited register").

(2) provisions specifying a form of words to be used by a registration officer for the purpose of -

(a) explaining to persons registered or applying to be registered, or persons acting on behalf of such persons, the purposes for which the full register and the edited register may be used, and

(b) ascertaining whether the exclusion of their names and addresses from the edited register is requested by or on behalf of such persons.

10A. Provisions requiring copies of the full register and other documents, or prescribed parts of them, to be available for inspection by the public at such places as may be prescribed.

10B. - (1) Provisions authorising or requiring a registration officer -

(a) to supply to such persons as may be prescribed copies of the full register and other documents, or prescribed parts of them, whether free of charge or on payment of a prescribed fee;

(b) to supply to any persons copies of the edited register, or any prescribed part of it, on payment of a prescribed fee.

(2) Provisions specifying, in relation to any description of persons prescribed by regulations made in pursuance of sub-paragraph (1)(a) above, the purposes for which copies supplied to such persons under such regulations, or information contained in them, may be used whether by such persons or by employees or other persons authorised by them in accordance with regulations to have access to such copies or information contained in them.

(3) Without prejudice to the generality of sub-paragraph (1) above or paragraph 11A below, regulations made in pursuance of sub-paragraph (1) may contain any such provisions as are authorised by paragraph 11A.

11. - (1) Provisions imposing prohibitions or restrictions relating to the extent (if any) to which -

(a) persons inspecting the full register in accordance with regulations made in pursuance of paragraph 10A above may make copies of the register;

(b) persons to whom copies of the full register are supplied (whether in accordance with regulations made in pursuance of paragraph 10B above or in accordance with any other provision made by or under an Act) may -

(i) supply those copies, or otherwise disclose any information contained in them, to other persons, or

(ii) make use of any such information otherwise than for any purposes specified in such regulations or (as the case may be) for which the copies have been supplied in accordance with any such provision.

(2) Provisions imposing, in relation to persons -

(a) to whom copies of the full register have been supplied, or information contained in such copies has been disclosed, in accordance with regulations made in pursuance of this paragraph, or

(b) who otherwise have access to such copies or information,

Prohibitions or restrictions corresponding to those which may be imposed by virtue of sub-paragraph (1) above.

(3) Provisions imposing, in relation to persons involved in the preparation of the full register, prohibitions with respect to supplying copies of the full register and disclosing information contained in it.

(4) In this paragraph any reference to the full register includes a reference to any part of it."

(3) In paragraph 13 (offences and supplemental matters), after sub-paragraph (1) there shall be inserted -

"(1A) Provisions making it an offence (punishable on summary conviction by a fine not exceeding level 5 on the standard scale) -

(a) for a person to contravene any regulations made in pursuance of paragraph 11 above or to do so in any prescribed circumstances, or

(b) where such contravention has occurred on the part of a person in the employment, or otherwise under the direction or control, of a company or other organisation, for -
(i) a director of a company, or
(ii) a person concerned with the management of the organisation,
To have failed to take such steps as it was reasonable for him to take to secure the operation of procedures designed to prevent, so far as reasonably practicable, the occurrence of such contraventions on the part of such persons."

Part II
CONDUCT OF ELECTIONS
New electoral procedures
10. Pilot schemes for local elections in England and Wales.
11. Revision of procedures in the light of pilot schemes.
Manner of voting
12. Changes relating to absent voting at elections in Great Britain.
Persons with disabilities
13. Assistance with voting for persons with disabilities.

Part III
MISCELLANEOUS AND GENERAL
Miscellaneous
14. Free delivery of election addresses at Greater London Authority elections.
General
15. Minor and consequential amendments and repeals.
16. Financial provisions.
17. Citation, construction, commencement and extent.
SCHEDULES:
Schedule 1 - Registration: amendments of 1983 Act.
Schedule 2 - Registration: overseas electors.
Schedule 3 - Registration: local elections in Northern Ireland.
Schedule 4 - Absent voting in Great Britain.

Schedule 5 - Free delivery of election addresses at first GLA mayoral election:
New Schedule 3A to the greater London Authority Act 1999.
Schedule 6 - Minor and consequential amendments.
Schedule 7 - Repeals.
Part I - Repeals extending to whole of the United Kingdom.
Part II - Repeals extending to England, Wales and Scotland.
Part III - Repeals extending to Northern Ireland only.

The Representation of the People Act is Crown copyright and was obtained from the website shown below.
In the above Act, part I, is shown in full.
Due to lack of space within this book, the remainder of the Act is summarised only. A full copy of the Act 2000 can be viewed on the web at:- www.homeoffice.gov.uk
A copy can be purchased online or direct from Her Majesty's Stationery Office.

20

STATUTORY AND LEGAL SOURCES AND FURTHER READING

Primary legislation governing elections

The Local Government Act 1972
Specifies term of office of members of local authorities; qualifications and disqualifications for holding office on a local authority; filling casual vacancies.

The House of Commons Disqualification Act 1975
Lists offices, the holders of which are disqualified from membership of the House of Commons; amended and reprinted from time to time.

The European Parliamentary Elections Act 1978
Makes provisions for the election of Members of the European Parliament; lays down the number of members for England, Scotland, Wales and Northern Ireland.

European Parliament (Pay and Pensions) Act 1979
Makes provisions for the payment of the salaries and pensions of UK Members of the European Parliament.

Representation of the People Act 1981
Disqualifies certain convicted people from being elected to or sitting in the House of Commons.

The Representation of the People Act 1983
The principal Representation of the People Act, deals with the franchise, registration of electors, conduct of parliamentary and local elections, election expenses, candidates and agents, offences, election petitions. The parliamentary elections rules

are set out in Schedule 1.

Representation of the People Act 1985
Introduced voting rights for British citizens overseas (for up to 5 years); introduced new provisions on absent voting; increased the deposit from £150 to £500; provides for the combination of polls and the filling of seats on a council when there are insufficient nominations; makes a number of miscellaneous amendments to the 1983 Act.

Local Government Act 1985
Contains certain disqualifications from being a member of a local authority (Part IV of the Act).

European Communities (Amendment) Act 1986
Amended references to the European Assembly to become references to the European Parliament.

Representation of the People Act 1989
Increased the qualifying period for British citizens overseas from 5 to 20 years: enfranchised British citizens who went abroad before they were old enough to register as electors; introduced a 4:1 differential between candidates' expenses at parliamentary by-elections and general elections.

Local Government and Housing Act 1989
Makes provisions for the disqualification and political restriction of certain officers and staff.

Representation of the People Act 1990
Allowed an absent vote for an indefinite period to electors no longer resident at their qualifying address.

Representation of the People Act 1991
Amended section 29 of the 1983 Act to place the reimbursement of returning officers' charges on a more efficient and workable basis.

Local Government Act 1992
Establishes the Local Government Commission for England in place of the Local Government Boundary Commission for England.

Boundary Commissions Act 1992
Amended Parliamentary Constituencies Act 1986 to set new deadline of 31 Dec 1994 for the fourth general review of constituencies and shortened the interval between future reviews to eight to twelve years.

European Parliamentary Elections Act 1993
Provides a mechanism for the initial redrawing of the European Parliamentary constituency boundaries in England and Wales to accommodate six additional seats allocated to the United Kingdom.

Local Government (Wales) Act 1994
Establishes new local government areas in Wales.

Secondary legislation governing elections
The Returning Officers (Parliamentary Constituencies) (England and Wales) Order 1983
Designates the returning officers and acting returning officers for parliamentary constituencies in England and Wales.

The Representation of the People Regulations 1986
Makes detailed provision about the compilation of the register, registration as a service voter, voluntary patient or overseas elector, the claims procedures, publication and supply of the register, absent voting applications, issue and receipt of postal ballot papers and the combination of polls; prescribes a number of electoral registration and election forms.

The European Parliamentary Elections Regulations 1986
Applies, for the purpose of European Parliamentary elections

the Representation of the People Act 1983 and the Representation of the People Regulations 1986.

The Local Elections (Principal Areas) Rules 1986
Provides for the conduct of county, district and London borough council elections in England and Wales; correspond to the Parliamentary Elections Rules (Schedule 1 to the 1983 Act).

The Local Elections (Parishes and Communities) Rules 1986
Applies similarly to parish and community councils in England and Wales.

The Parish and Community Meetings (Polls) Rules 1987
Provide for the conduct of a poll consequent upon a parish or community meeting.

The Transfer of Functions (Returning Officers' Charges) Order 1991
Transfers responsibility for the setting and reimbursement of returning officers' fees and charges from the Treasury to the Home Department.

The Returning Officers' Accounts (Parliamentary Elections) (England and Wales) Regulations 1991
Provides for the time and manner in which a returning officer's account, are to be submitted.

The European Parliamentary Constituencies (England) Order 1994
Specifies the composition of European Parliamentary constituencies in England.

The Representation of the People (Variation of Limits of Candidates' Election Expenses) Order 1994
Prescribes the maximum amounts of a candidate's expenses at a parliamentary or local election.

The European Parliamentary Elections (Returning Officers) (England and Wales) Order 1994
Designates the parliamentary constituencies which provide the returning officers at European Parliamentary elections in England and Wales.

The Parliamentary Elections (Returning Officers' Charges) Order 1994
Specifies the fees and reasonable charges for acting returning officers at a parliamentary election.

The European Elections (Returning Officers' Charges) Order 1994
Specifies the fees and reasonable charges for acting returning officers at European parliamentary election.

The European Parliamentary (United Kingdom Representatives) Pensions (Consolidation and Amendment) Pensions Order 1994
Makes detailed provision for the payment of pensions to UK Members of the European Parliament.

The Returning Officers' Accounts (European Parliamentary Elections) (England and Wales) Regulations 1994
Provides for the time when and manner in which the account of a returning officer at European Parliamentary election is to be submitted.

Some of the rules and regulations listed above have been amended by:-
The Local Elections (Parishes and Communities) (Amendment) Rules 1987

The Local Elections (Principal Areas) (Amendment) Rules 1987

The Parish and Communities Meetings (Polls) (Amendment) Rules 1987

The European Parliamentary Constituencies (England) (Miscellaneous Changes) Order 1989

The European Parliamentary Constituencies (Wales) (Miscellaneous Changes) Order 1989

The Local Elections (Parishes and Communities) (Amendment) Rules 1990

The Local Elections (Principal Areas) (Amendment) Rules 1990

The Representation of the People (Amendment) Regulations 1990

The Local Elections (Parishes and Communities) (Amendment) Rules 1990

The European Parliamentary Elections (Amendment) Regulations 1990

The Returning Officers (Parliamentary Constituencies) (England and Wales) (Amendment) Order 1991

The Representation of the People (Amendment) Regulations 1991

The European Parliamentary Election (Amendment) Regulations 1991

The Representation of the People (Amendment) Regulations 1992

The European Parliamentary Election (Amendment) Regulations 1992

The European Parliamentary Election (Amendment) Regulations 1994

This list is not exhaustive and some of it has been repealed by the 2000 Act. It does not include the corresponding Scotland and Northern Ireland orders and regulations, orders relating to boundary changes, the various Welsh forms or orders to local elections made by the Department of the Environment.

Textbooks

Returning officers researching any point of election law will usually start with either of the two works referred to below, depending which type of election they are dealing with at the time. Schofield's is a reference work which covers all types of election, whereas Parker's previous editions were more specialised, covering only Parliamentary elections but in volumes after 1995 they now cover all the other types of election.

Parker's Conduct of Parliamentary Elections & The Conduct of European Elections. Published by Charles Knight & Company Ltd 25 New Street Square, London EC4A 3JA.

Schofield's Election Law Edited by A.J. Little, solicitor. Published by Shaw & Sons Ltd, Shaway House, Lower Sydenham, London SE26 5AB.

Case Law

To quite a large extent the election process has been built up over the years using references to previous cases and they have set a precedent for similar types of action. This has come about because sometimes an Act of Parliament does not or is not specific on a particular part of the legislation. It then falls upon the courts to make a decision. There are many such cases referred to in the above works.

21

THE ELECTORAL REGIONS

The Electoral Regions

Scotland, geographical area: Scotland, electorate, 4,015,399. Number of Members of the European Parliament: 8

Northern Ireland, geographical area: Northern Ireland, electorate 1,202,929. Number of Members of the European Parliament: 3.

North East, geographical area: former county of Cleveland, Durham, Northumbria, former county of Tyne & Wear, electorate, 1,969,966. Number of Members of the European Parliament: 4.

Yorkshire and the Humber, geographical area: former counties of Humberside, North Yorkshire, South Yorkshire, West Yorkshire, electorate, 3,795,388. Number of Members of the European Parliament: 7.

North West, geographical area: Cheshire, Cumbria, boroughs within Greater Manchester, Lancashire, former Metropolitan county of Merseyside, electorate, 5,209,540. Number of Members of the European Parliament: 10.

East Midlands, geographical area: Derbyshire, Leicestershire, Lincolnshire, Northamptonshire, Nottinghamshire, electorate, 3,195,665. Number of Members of the European Parliament: 6.

West Midlands, geographical area: Hereford and Worcester, Shropshire, Staffordshire, Warwickshire, former Metropolitan county of West Midlands, electorate 4,034,992. Number of Members of the European Parliament: 8.

Wales, geographical area: Wales, electorate, 2,229,826. Number of Members of the European Parliament: 5.

Eastern, geographical area: Bedfordshire, Cambridgeshire, Essex, Hertfordshire, Norfolk, Suffolk, electorate, 4,053,900. Number of Members of the European Parliament: 8.

London, geographical area: London boroughs, the City of London, electorate, 4,972,495. Number of Members of the European Parliament: 10.

South West, geographical area: former county of Avon, Cornwall, Devon, Dorset, Gloucestershire, Scilly Isles, Somerset, Wiltshire, electorate, 3,777,497. Number of Members of the European Parliament: 7.

South East, geographical area: Berkshire, Buckinghamshire, East Sussex, Hampshire, Isle of Wight, Kent, Oxfordshire, Surrey, West Sussex, electorate, 6,023,991. Number of Members of the European Parliament: 11.

22

GLOSSARY

Absent voter: A postal or proxy vote for people who cannot vote in person at the polling station.

Acting returning officer: At parliamentary or European elections, the officer in charge of the election.

Ballot: The means of election by one vote per elector.

Ballot papers: The paper required to allow the voter to cast his vote by making a mark against the preferred candidate.

By-election: An election to fill a vacancy created by, e.g. the resignation or death of a councillor or Member of Parliament.

Candidate: Someone who completes a form of nomination in the hope of being elected.

Canvasser: Someone who acts on behalf of a candidate or agent, visiting electors or on behalf of the registration officer to collect information for the register of electors.

Case law: Previous cases where legislation has not covered a particular point but courts have made a ruling that will subsequently be followed.

Claims for inclusion: Are additional applications made to register after the publication date.

Combined election: Where two elections are held on the same day. Eg: parliamentary general and local council.

Committee: A group of Councillors or other such people elected to serve either a council or a club etc.

Constituency: Divisions by which the country is divided for the purpose of electing Members of Parliament.

Corrections of Register: Made if the register does not comply with the wishes of the Electoral Registration officer, under certain conditions.

Counting agents: Anyone appointed by the candidate or election agent to oversee the counting of the votes on the occasion of an election.

County Council: A council for the whole of a county made up of district councils.

Data: A print or information, usually derived from a computer.

Dies non: A day not counted in calculating the election timetable.

Disqualification: Prevents the election of a Member or candidate.

District council: Another name for a borough council.

Draft: A pre-copy of the register is called a draft: it is produced before the main register.

Election: The means of democratic selection of candidates.

General election: Another name for Parliamentary elections.

Guidance: Notice to guide voters at the polling stations as to the method of voting.

In Charge: The officer supervising the counting of the votes at an election.

Junk mail: The term used for unsolicited mailing shots or advertising mail.

Local elections: County or district elections.

Maximum: The amounts of expenses etc., above the limits of which candidates are not allowed to spend.

Member countries: Countries that make up the European Union.

Nomination: The form completed by anyone wishing to be a candidate at an election.

Overseas electors: People who live out of the UK and are allowed to vote in Parliamentary or European elections for a specified time.

Parish: A political division of a county for local civil government.

Parliamentary election: An election for Members of Parliament, also known as a general election.

Petition: An objection to an election can only be dealt with by an election court, to invoke this action a petition would have to be presented.

Polling day: The day set aside for the electorate to cast their votes.

Postal votes: Votes for people not able to vote at the polling station also referred to as absent votes.

Presiding officer: The officer in charge of a polling station.

Primary legislation: The main form of legislation: Acts of Parliament.

Proxy vote: Someone who is going to be out of the UK on Election Day can appoint another to act on his behalf (a proxy)

Publication: Notices or posters advertising certain parts of the election, notice of poll.

Regions: The divisions of the electorate areas for European Parliamentary Elections.

Register of electors: The means of recording the names of people who are eligible to vote.

Respondent: The person against who certain court cases including electoral petitions are brought.

Returning officer: The officer in charge of an election.

Revocation: To remove from office.

Secondary legislation: Legislation produced as a supplement to the Acts of Parliament: also known as statutory instruments.

Security for costs: A payment by a petitioner into court in case a costs order is subsequently made against him.

Sub-agent: An election agent appointed by the election agent to cover a separate part of a constituency.

Timetable: Means of working out the required number of days for an election.

Unitary authority: A new description of local councils after the dissolution of the county councils.

Voting: The method by which the electorate use their democratic right to cast their vote for a selected candidate.

Writ: A written order in the name of the Crown which commands the person to whom it is addressed to perform a stated act: in the event of a general election it would be addressed to the returning officer.

INDEX

FORMS REQUIRED WITH SOME SPECIMENS

The various forms required

Timetable (specimen as used for local government elections)

Timetable (specimen as used for Parliamentary General Elections)

Notice of election (specimen poster which has to be displayed at the commencement of each election).

Appointment of election agent. (to be completed by candidate appointing his/her election agent)

Nomination paper. (To be completed by the candidate or his/her election agent)

Candidates consent to nomination. (This form to be completed by the candidate, consenting to his/her nomination, the previous paper is invalid without this).

Statement as to persons nominated. (Must be published showing all the candidates full names, addresses and description if any).

Notice of particulars of election agents. (Must be published on a specified day showing the name, address and office address of all the election agents complete with the name of the candidate for whom they are agents).

Ballot Paper. (specimen as used for local government elections).

The requirement of secrecy, specimen document as handed out to everyone who is involved in local elections a modified version of which is handed out at Parliamentary Elections.

Declaration by candidate as to election expenses. (Must be completed by the candidate or the election agent and signed by the candidate in the presence of a Justice of the Peace or proper officer of a Council, who must witness the signature).

Declaration by agent as to election expenses. (Must be completed and signed by the election agent, witnessed by a Justice of the Peace or proper officer of a Council).

Return of election expenses. (Must be a true record of all expenses and signed by whoever is making the claim).

Register cover. (The cover as has been used for the register of electors each year).

Declaration of Acceptance of Office. (This is a form that must be completed before any successful candidate can perform any duties or sit in council or on any committees).

Guidance of Voters (notice) a copy or copies of which must be displayed at every polling station on Election Day

Specimen timetable as used for local elections on the 2nd May 1996.

ANY BOROUGH COUNCIL
Election of councillors for the borough of Any
TIMETABLE OF PROCEEDINGS

Publication of notice of election.　　　Not later than Monday 25th
　　　　　　　　　　　　　　　　　　March
　　　　　　　　(Twenty-fifth day before day of election)

Delivery of nomination papers　　　　Not later than NOON on
　　　　　　　　　　　　　　　　　　Tuesday 2nd April
　　　　　　　　(Nineteenth day before day of election)

Publication of statement of　　　　　Not later than NOON on
persons nominated....　　　　　　　　Tuesday 9th April
　　　　　　　　(Seventeenth day before day of election)

Delivery of notices of withdrawal　　) Not later than NOON on
of candidature....　　　　　　　　　　Wednesday 10th April
Notice of appointment of election　　) (Sixteenth day before day of
agents.....　　　　　　　　　　　　　) election)

Applications to be treated as　　　　Not later than NOON on
absent or proxy voters...　　　　　　Monday 15th April
　　　　　　　　(Thirteenth day before day of election)

Despatch of postal ballot papers...　　To be decided by the Returning
　　　　　　　　　　　　　　　　　　officer

Publication of notice of poll...   Wednesday 24th April
(Sixth day before day of election)

Applications to be treated as absent   Not later than NOON on
or proxy voters-sudden changes in   Wednesday 24th April
health or election employment...   (Sixth day before day of election)

Notice of appointment of polling   Thursday 25th April
or counting agents...   (Fifth day before day of election)

Polling....   Thursday 2nd May

Submission of return and   Not later than Thursday 6th
declaration of election expenses...   June 1996

Counting of the votes   Thursday 2nd May 1996

Specimen of Parliamentary timetable

Proclamation summoning new Parliament.
Dissolution of Parliament.
Issue of Writ.

Receipt of Writ...   Usually two days after proclamation

Publication of notice of election   4.00 p.m. two days after Writ
received

Receipt of absent voting applications Four days after proclamation

Delivery of nomination papers   ) 4.00 p.m. six days after procla-
Withdrawal of candidate   ) mation.
Appointment of election agents   ) (Between the hours of
10 a.m. & 4 p.m.)

Publication of statement of persons   Six days after proclamation
nominated
(Published at close of time for making objections or as soon as any
objections are disposed of.)

Receipt of late absent votes on health   Five days after nomination day
grounds

Appointments of polling and counting   Nine days after nomination day
agents, publication of notice

Day of poll   Eleven days after nomination
day (7.00 a.m. to 10.00 p.m.)

Return of declaration of candidates'   Thirty-five days after the day on
election expenses   which the result was declared

Publication of time and place for   Ten working days after delivery
inspection of election expenses   of election expenses

Notice of Election (specimen poster)

Notice of Election

ELECTION OF A COUNCILLOR

FOR EACH OF THE ELECTORAL WARDS OF THE BOROUGH OF READING

1. An election is to be held of ONE Councillor for each of the following Electoral Wards, namely - ABBEY, BATTLE, CAVERSHAM, CHURCH, KATESGROVE, KENTWOOD, MINSTER, NORCOT, PARK, PEPPARD, REDLANDS, SOUTHCOTE, THAMES, TILEHURST, and WHITLEY of the Borough of Reading.

2. Nomination papers must be delivered at the office of the Returning Officer, Mr R.C. Taylor, Civic Offices, Reading, on any day after the date of this notice, but not later than NOON on TUESDAY 4th April 1995.

3. Forms of nomination paper may be obtained at the said office of the Returning Officer, who will, at the request of any elector for the said wards, prepare a nomination paper for signature.

4. If the election is contested, the poll will take place on THURSDAY 4th May 1995.

5. Electors and their proxies should take note that applications to be treated as an absent voter and other applications and notices about postal or proxy voting must reach the Electoral Registration Officer at the Civic Centre, Reading, RG1 7TD by NOON on WEDNESDAY 12th April 1995 if they are to be effective for these elections.

6. Applications to be treated as an absent voter due to unforeseen illness must reach the Electoral Registration Officer by NOON on WEDNESDAY 26th April 1995 if they are to be effective for these elections.

27th March 1995   R. C. Taylor, Returning Officer

Printed by Reading Borough Council   Published by R. C. Taylor
Reprographics Department   Returning Officer, Civic Centre, Reading

---

Appointment of election agent (specimen form)

ANY BOROUGH COUNCIL ELECTION

Day of Election..........................

To...............................

Notice of Appointment of Election Agent

I

of

a candidate at the above mentioned election HEREBY GIVE YOU NOTICE that I have appointed

of

to be my agent for such election.

The address of my election agent's office to which all claims, notices, writs, summonses and documents may be sent is:-

Dated this   day of   2001.

(Signed)...
Candidate at this election

I HEREBY ACCEPT the above appointment.

Dated this   day of   2001.

(Signed)..
Election Agent

NOTE:- This notice must be delivered to the proper office of the Council not later than NOON on the SIXTEENTH day before day of election.

In computing any period of time for this purpose, Saturday, Sunday, Christmas Eve, Christmas Day, Maundy Thursday, Good Friday, Bank Holiday or day appointed for public thanksgiving or mourning must be disregarded.

Printed by the Returning officer Any Borough Council

Nomination Paper

ELECTION OF A COUNCILLOR
for the   Ward
of the Borough of Any Town
Day of Election...................

We, the undersigned, being local government electors for the said ward do hereby nominate the under-mentioned person as a candidate at the said election.

Candidate's Surname	Other names in full	Description (if any)	Home address in full
SIGNATURES		Electoral Number (see note 3) Distinctive Letters/number	

Proposer.....................................   ....
Seconder.....................................   ....
We the undersigned, being local government electors for
the said ward, do hereby assent to the foregoing nomination.

1. ....
2. ....
3. ....
4. ....
5. ....
6. ....
7. ....
8. ....

NOTE

1. The attention of candidates and electors is drawn to the rules for filling up nomination papers and other provisions relating to nomination contained in election rules in Schedule 2 to the Local Election (Principal Areas) Rules 1986.

2. Where a candidate is commonly known by some title he/she may be described by his/her title as if it were his/her surname.

3. A person's electoral number is his/her number in the register to be used at the election (including the distinctive letter of the Parliamentary polling district in which he/she is registered) except that before publication of the register his/her number (if any) in the electors lists for that shall be used instead.

4. An elector may not -
(a) subscribe more nomination papers than there are vacancies to be filled in the electoral area in which the election is held; or
(b) subscribe a nomination paper for more than one electoral area in the same district or London Borough.

5. A person whose name is entered in the register or electors lists may not subscribe a nomination paper if the entry gives as the date on which he/she will become of voting age a date later than the day fixed for the poll.

Printed and published by the Returning officer of Any Borough Council.

Any Borough Council

ELECTION OF COUNCILLOR(S)
For...........................Ward
Day of election..................

CANDIDATES CONSENT TO NOMINATION
(To be given on or within one month before the last day for the delivery of nomination papers, and delivered at the place and within the time for delivery of nomination papers).

1. (name in full) ....of (home address in full) ....
hereby consent to my nomination as a candidate for election as councillor for
the...ward of
the...

I declare that on that day of my nomination I am qualified and that, if there is a poll on the day of election, I will be qualified to be so elected by virtue of being on that day or those days a Commonwealth citizen, European Union citizen or citizen of the Republic of Ireland, who has attained the age of 21 years and that
   (a) I am registered as a local government elector for the area of the Borough
named above in respect of (qualifying address in full)
....
and my electoral number (see note below)
is...........................; or
(b) I have during the whole of the twelve months preceding that day or those days occupied as owner or tenant the following land or other premises in that area (description of land or premises) ....
.... or
   (c) My principal or only place of work during those twelve

months has been in that area at (give address of place of work
and, where appropriate, name of employer).........................;or
(**d**) I have during the whole of those twelve months resided
in that area at (give address in full) ....
....

I declare that to the best of my knowledge and belief I am not disqualified for being elected by reason of any disqualification set out in
Section 80 of the Local Government Act 1972, a copy of which is printed overleaf, and I do not hold a politically restricted post, within the
meaning of Part 1 of the Local Government and Housing Act 1989,
under a local authority within the meaning of that Part.

Signed..

Date..

Signed in my presence

Signature of witness.....................................

Name and address of witness...
....

* Delete whichever is appropriate

Note:- A person's electoral number is his/her number in the register to
be used at the election (including the distinctive letter of the
Parliamentary polling district in which he/she is registered) except that
before publication of the register his/her number (if any) in the electors
lists for that register shall be used instead.

Printed and published by the Returning officer, Any Borough Council.

---

*The reverse side of the consent to nomination form would show extracts
from the Local Government Act 1972 - Part V (as amended). Also included with the consent form would be a form of Registration of political parties and a certificate to be signed by the candidate for the registration of
a party or a party emblem, if any.*

*Within the form of the certificate, the candidate is reminded that they
may not use a description, which is likely to lead voters to associate them
with a political party unless the description is authorised by a certificate
issued by the party's registered nominating officer. Any other candidates
would enter a description of "Independent", or no description at all.*

Notice of particulars of election agents

BOROUGH OF ANY

I hereby give notice that the following names and addresses of election agents of candidates at this election, and the addresses of the offices of such election agents Nominated for which all claims, notices, writs, summonses, and other documents addressed to them may be sent, have respectively been, or deemed to have been, declared in writing to me as follows: ward

Name of Candidate	Name of Agent	Address of Election Agent	Office of election agent, notices, writs etc., may be sent

Dated this   day of April 2001

Returning officer..

Statement as to persons nominated (specimen form)

BOROUGH OF ANY
The following is a statement as to the persons
Nominated for Election as a Borough Councillor for the
Ward

Persons Nominated

Ward	Surname (in full)	Other names (if any)	Description	Home address	Proposer's name	Decision of Returning Officer that nomination paper is invalid or other reason a person nominated no longer stands nominated
1	2	3	4	5	6	7

The persons opposite whose names no entry is made in column 7 have been and stand validly nominated.

Dated this   day of April 2001
Returning Officer................................

The above form must be completed and displayed by the Returning Officer on the day and date specified in the election timetable, a copy of which should have been given to each election agent or candidate.

Specimen ballot paper

Counterfoil No.	VOTE FOR ONE CANDIDATE ONLY	
	BLACK 1. Stephen Alan Black 1 The Knoll, Any Town - on sea The Opinion Poll Party	
	BROWN 2. Charlie Harold Brown 5 Under the Arches Road, Any Town The National Lottery Party	
	GREEN 3. Edward Arthur Green (known as Ed) 2 Blackthorn Drive, Any Town The Mad Hatters Tea Party	

The names have been changed to protect the innocent

All joking aside, it is required by the statute that the ballot papers are set out in such a way that no unfair advantage is given to any one candidate. You will notice that the names are in alphabetical order descending down the page. All surnames are in upper case and bold letters, with the full name below it. The address of the candidate is also shown in full, although the post code need not be included. The last item on the paper is the description of the candidate, this can be the party or an "Independent" or need not have any description at all.

The spaces between the names and the type face must be the same for all candidates. If there were more than one vacancy the heading would be changed accordingly.

There follows a specimen form, as issued to every person engaged in election work, be it returning officer, presiding officer, poll clerk, counting assistant, candidate, agent or any others at polling stations or at the counting of the votes. This form in years gone by, had to have the signature witnessed by a Justice of the Peace. All that is required now is that when questioned, a declaration can be made that the form has been read.

ELECTION OF COUNCILLORS

To persons attending at the taking of the poll or the counting of the votes at this election
Your attention is drawn to the provisions of section 66, sub-sections (1), (2), (3) and (6) of the Representation of the People Act 1983, which are set out below.
These provisions concern the maintaining of secrecy of the voting and should be read carefully before you attend at any polling station or at the counting of the votes.

REPRESENTATION OF THE PEOPLE ACT, 1983

(1) The following persons -
   (a) every returning officer and every presiding officer or poll clerk attending at a polling station;
   (b) every candidate or election agent or polling agent so attending; shall maintain and aid in maintaining the secrecy of voting and shall not, except for some purpose authorized by law, communicate to any person before the poll is closed any information as to -
(i) the name of any elector or proxy for an elector who has or has not applied for a ballot paper or voted at a polling station;
(ii) the number on the register of electors of any elector who, or whose proxy, has or has not applied for a ballot paper or voted at a polling station; or
(iii) the official mark.

(2) Every person attending at the counting of the votes shall maintain and aid in maintaining the secrecy of voting and shall not -
   (a) ascertain or attempt to ascertain at the counting of the votes

the number on the back of any ballot paper;

(b) communicate any information obtained at the counting of the votes as to the candidate for whom any vote is given on any particular ballot paper.

(3) No person shall -

(a) interfere with or attempt to interfere with a voter when recording his/her vote;

(b) obtain or attempt to obtain in a polling station information as to the candidate for whom a voter in that station is about to vote or has voted;

(c) communicate at any time to any person any information obtained in a polling station as to the candidate for whom a voter in that station is about to vote or has voted, or as to the number on the back of the ballot paper given to a voter at that station;

(d) directly or indirectly induce a voter to display his ballot paper after he has marked it so as to make known to any person the name of the candidate for whom he has or has not voted.

(6) If any person acts in contravention of this section, he/she shall be liable on summary conviction to a fine not exceeding level 5 on the standard scale or imprisonment for a term not exceeding six months.

Printed and published by the Returning officer, Any Borough Council

Declaration by the candidate as to election expenses

ELECTION OF COUNCILLORS

For the   ward of the Borough of Any
Date of Publication of Notice of Election..................20
Name of Candidate....................................

Declaration by Candidate as to Expenses
I,
of
DO SOLEMNLY AND SINCERELY DECLARE as follows:-
1. I am the person named above as candidate at this election (and was my own election agent).
2. I have examined the return of election expenses (about to be) delivered by (me) (my election agent) to the Returning officer, of which a copy is now shown to me and marked, and to the best of my knowledge and belief it is a complete and correct return as required by law.
3. To the best of my knowledge and belief, all expenses shown in the return as paid were paid by (me) (my election agent), except as otherwise stated in relation to my personal expenses.
4. I understand that the law does not allow any election expenses not mentioned in this return to be defrayed except in pursuance of a court order.

Signed_____
Signed and declared by the above-named declarant
on the..........day of...............20 ..
before me,
Signed
(Description)...
Note:- Delete words in brackets which are not applicable.

Where there has been a change of election agent, suitable variations may be introduced into the declaration as to expenses.
*This declaration may be made either before a justice of the peace or before any person who is chairman of the inner London Education Authority, a county council or district council or mayor of a London borough or before the proper officer of any such council.

Printed and published by the Returning officer, Any Borough Council, Any town.

Declaration by election agent as to election expenses

ELECTION OF COUNCILLORS
For the   Ward of the Borough of Any
Date of Publication of Notice of Election.................2001
Name of Candidate................................
Declaration by Election Agent as to Expenses
I, ...of...
DO SOLEMNLY AND SINCERELY DECLARE as follows:-
1. I was at this election the election agent of the person named above as a candidate.
2. I have examined the return of election expenses delivered by me to the Returning officer, of which a copy is now shown to me and marked, and to the best of my knowledge and belief it is a complete and correct return as required by law.
3. To the best of my knowledge and belief, all expenses shown in the return as paid were paid by me, except as otherwise stated in relation to the candidates personal expenses.
4. I understand that the law does not allow any election expenses not mentioned in this return to be defrayed except in pursuance of a court order.
Signature of declarant................................
Signed and declared by the above-named declarant
on the..........day of...............2001
before me,
(Signed)...
(Description)...
Note:- Delete words in brackets which are not applicable.
Where there has been a change of election agent, suitable variations may be introduced into the declaration as to expenses.
*This declaration may be made either before a Justice of the Peace or before any person who is chairman of the inner London Education Authority, a county council or district council or mayor of a London borough or before the proper officer of any such council.

Printed and published by the Returning officer, Any Borough Council

Return of election expenses

ELECTION OF COUNCILLORS
For the   Ward of the Borough of Any
Date of publication of Notice of Election..............2001
Name of Candidate....................................
RETURN OF ELECTION EXPENSES
I,
of
(am the election agent of the person named above as a candidate at this election) (am the person named above as candidate at this election and was my own election agent).*

I hereby make the following return of (the candidate's) (my) election expenses at this election.

RECEIPTS

Note:- Include all money, securities or equivalent of money received in respect of expenses incurred on account of or in connection with or incidental to the above election.

+ Received of the above-named candidate
+ Paid by me (if the candidate is his/her own election agent) £
Received of:-
Delete words in brackets which are not applicable.   £

Where there has been a change of election agent, suitable variations may be introduced here and elsewhere in the return.

+ Delete whichever is applicable.

:- Here set out separately the name and description of each person, club, society or association and the amount received from him/her or them.

Printed and published by the Returning officer, Any Borough Council.

EXPENDITURE

Note:- The return must deal under separate heading or sub-heading with any expenses included therein as respects which a return is required to be made by section 75 of the Representation of the People Act 1983. Candidate's personal expenses:-

Paid by (him/her) (me as candidate)	£
Paid by me (acting as my election agent)	£
Received by me for my services as election agent (a)	£
*+ Paid to (as) polling agent (as per annexed list)	£
*+ Paid to (as) clerk (messenger)	£
for days service (as per annexed list)	£
*+ Paid to the (following) persons (named in the annexed list) in respect of goods supplied or work or labour done (b)	£
*+ Paid to (as) speaker(s) at public meeting(s) (as per annexed list) (at on 2001) as (remuneration) (expenses)	£
*+ Paid for the hire of rooms:-	
for holding public meetings (as per annexed list) (paid to for hire of ©)	£
for committee rooms (as per annexed list) (paid to for hire of ©)	£
Paid for postage	£
Paid for telegrams	£
*+ Paid for miscellaneous matters (as per annexed list) (to d)	£
	£

In addition to the above I am aware ((a) as election agent for the above-named candidate) of the following disputed and unpaid claims:-

Disputed claims:-

*by   for (e)

Unpaid claims allowed by the court to be paid after the proper time or in respect of which application has been or is about to be made to the   court (f):-

*by   for (g)   £

Signature of person making the claim.................................

(j) Set out separately the name and description of each person with the amount paid to or claimed by him/her.

+ These particulars may be set out in a separate list annexed to the account.

(k) Omit if candidate is his/her own election agent.

(b) Set out the nature of the goods supplied or work and labour done thus (printing), (advertising), (stationery).

© Identify the rooms by naming or describing them.

(d) Set out the reason for the payment.

(e) Set out the goods, work and labour or other matter on the ground of which the claim is based.

(f) State in each case whether the High Court, or some other court.

(g) Set out the goods, work and labour or other matter on account of which the claim is due.

Specimen Register Cover *(used up to the elections in May 2000. The last qualifying date as shown below will cease to be used after the Act of 2000 comes into force, in March 2001)*

BOROUGH OF BRACKNELL FOREST
EUROPEAN PARLIAMENTARY REGION: SOUTH EAST
PARLIAMENTARY CONSTITUENCY: BRACKNELL
BOROUGH WARD: BINFIELD
PARISH/TOWN (WARD): BINFIELD
POLLING DISTRICT LA
REGISTER OF ELECTORS
(QUALIFYING DATE 10th of OCTOBER 2000)
IN FORCE FROM 16th FEBRUARY 2001

NOTE: The date printed immediately before an elector's name indicates the date on which he/she reaches voting age and that he/she will be able to vote at elections held on or after that date.

E Printed before a name indicates that the Elector is entitled to vote at European Parliamentary Elections ONLY.

F Printed before a name indicates that the Elector is entitled to vote at Parliamentary and European Parliamentary Elections ONLY.

G Printed before a name indicates that the Elector is a relevant citizen of the European Union and is entitled to vote at Local Government Elections ONLY.

K Printed before a name indicates that the Elector is a relevant citizen of the European Union and is entitled to vote at Local Government and European Parliamentary Elections ONLY.

U printed before a name indicates that the Elector is a relevant citizen of the European Union and is entitled to vote at European Parliamentary Elections ONLY.

Address of council offices	Insert: Name of officer
	Electoral Registration Officer
Telephone: Insert number	15th February 2001

Printed and published by the Electoral Registration Officer, Borough Council

Specimen of acceptance of office of Councillor.

Declaration of Acceptance of Office

I,
having been elected to the office of*
HEREBY DECLARE that I take that office upon myself, and will duly and faithfully fulfil the duties of it according to the best of my judgement and ability.
I undertake to be guided by the National Code of Local Government Conduct in the performance of my functions in that office.
Date   Signed_____

This declaration was made and signed before me
(signed)_____

+ Proper Officer of the Council
of the

----

* Insert description of office
+ If the declaration is made and subscribed before any other person authorized by section 83 (3) of the Local Government Act 1972, adapt accordingly

DIRECTIONS FOR THE GUIDANCE
OF VOTERS IN VOTING

---

1. When you are given a ballot paper make sure it is stamped with the official mark.

2. Go to one of the compartments. Mark a cross (X) in the box on the right hand side of the ballot paper opposite the name of the candidate you are voting for.

3. Fold the ballot paper in two. Show the official mark to the presiding officer, but do not let anyone see your vote. Put the ballot paper in the ballot box and leave the polling station.

4. Vote for ONE candidate only. Put no other mark on the ballot paper, or your vote may not be counted.

5. If by mistake you spoil a ballot paper, show it to the presiding officer and ask for another one.

The printer, publisher and Returning officer, address

The above guidance notes will be displayed in each of the polling stations for the direction and guidance of the electorate in voting.

NOTES